Your Life in Christ

George MacDonald

Edited by Michael Phillips

Books by Michael Phillips

Is Jesus Coming Back As Soon As We Think?
Make Me Like Jesus
God, A Good Father
Jesus, An Obedient Son
Destiny Junction
Kings Crossroads
Angels Watching Over Me
A Perilous Proposal
Dream of Freedom
Rift in Time
Hidden in Time
The Eleventh Hour
Legend of the Celtic Stone
An Ancient Strife
Your Life in Christ (George MacDonald)
George MacDonald: Scotland's Beloved Storyteller

Your Life in Christ

George MacDonald

Edited by Michael Phillips

BETHANY HOUSE
Minneapolis, Minnesota

Published by Bethany House Publishers
11400 Hampshire Avenue South
Bloomington, Minnesota 55438

Bethany House Publishers is a division of
Baker Publishing Group, Grand Rapids, Michigan.

Printed in the United States of America

Library of Congress Cataloging-in-Publication Data

MacDonald, George, 1824–1905.
    Your life in Christ : the nature of God and his work in human hearts / by
George MacDonald and Michael Phillips.
        p.   cm.
    Summary: "In this book drawn from MacDonald's sermons and published
essays, Michael Phillips makes MacDonald's wisdom and insights accessible
to today's readers. This volume explores topics that comprise the heart of
Christian theology, including 'The Creation in Christ,' 'Life,' 'Self-Denial,'
'Freedom,' and more"—Provided by publisher.
    ISBN 0-7642-0082-8 (pbk.)
    1. Christian life. I. Phillips, Michael R., 1946- II. Title.
    BV4501.3.M227   2005
    248.4—dc22   2005005232

Contents

Introduction

In England during the latter half of the nineteenth century, men of letters—novelists, poets, essayists, historians, journalists—occupied a prestigious rank near the top of society. It was the authors of the Victorian era who provided entertainment for the masses and who went "on tour" to speak in packed auditoriums, much like musicians and other celebrities today.

One of the most eminent of these was a Scotsman by the name of George MacDonald (1824–1905)—novelist, poet, author of fantasy and children's stories, and preacher—whose following was so widespread on both sides of the Atlantic that when he toured the Eastern and Midwestern United States in 1872–73, full halls greeted him wherever he went, from Boston and New York to Chicago and St. Louis.

In the 1935 book *The Victorians and Their Reading* by Amy Cruse, an intriguing frontispiece includes MacDonald in a composite photograph along with eight other noted authors, among them Dickens, Thackeray, and Carlyle. The eight are known to any modern student of the period and their works familiar reading in undergraduate English literature classes. However, most students and professors in today's colleges and universities have never heard of the group's ninth member. Upon seeing the photo, their response might well be, "Who is George MacDonald?"

Richard Reis amplifies this curious dichotomy:

Such a question would not have occurred to most of MacDonald's contemporaries. Instead they might have expressed surprise to learn that he would be largely forgotten by the middle of the twentieth century. For throughout the final third of the nineteenth century, George MacDonald's works were bestsellers and his status as [writer and Christian] sage was secure. His novels sold, both in Great Britain and in the United States, by the hundreds of thousands of copies; his lectures were popular and widely attended; his poetry earned him at least passing consideration for the laureateship; and his reputation as a Christian teacher was vast. This . . . popularity alone makes MacDonald a figure of some significance in literary history. . . . In his own time MacDonald was esteemed by an impressive roster of English and American literary and religious leaders. He was among the closest friends of John Ruskin [, Lady Byron] and Charles Dodgson [Lewis Carroll]; and he moved as a peer in the company of Alfred Tennyson, Charles Kingsley, F. D. Maurice, R. W. Gilder, Harriet Beecher Stowe, Oliver Wendell Holmes, Samuel Clemens [Mark Twain], and H. W. Longfellow. All of them respected, praised, and encouraged him, yet his reputation has nearly vanished while theirs survives. . . .

[It is not] that MacDonald has been entirely

ignored in the twentieth century. Indeed, although he is little known among the general reading public, MacDonald has received considerable scholarly and critical attention. . . . G. K. Chesterton was among the earliest twentieth-century critics who found MacDonald's "message" of importance to the post-Victorian sensibility . . . [and] referred to MacDonald as "one of the three or four greatest men of the nineteenth century." Richard Reis, *George Mac-Donald* [New York: Twayne Publishers, 1972, 17–18]

Despite this acclaim, however, through the years of the twentieth century, MacDonald's reputation slowly dwindled. Though less pronounced, the same fate fell to many of his colleagues. Their names may still be known in university English departments, but their books do not fly off the shelves at Borders or Barnes & Noble. Not many were as fortunate as Dickens to remain household names.

MacDonald had two strikes against him that caused his twentieth-century drift into anonymity. The first he shared with most of his contemporaries. It was simply a product of the times—verbosity, or wordiness.

Theirs was a different era, with different literary tastes on the part of the public and different literary styles on the part of writers. Five-hundred, even seven-hundred-page books were commonplace, containing one hundred and one hundred fifty word complex, circuitous sentences. The pace of life moved more slowly. Readers, on the whole more classically literate at the upper levels of society, were not only accustomed to it, they had the time and inclination to enjoy such writing. Another very practical consideration did not reward brevity—many novels were originally published in serialized form, for which authors were paid by the word.

MacDonald's writing possessed yet another quality, however, which distinguished it from that of his peers. This factor undoubtedly caused him to be forgotten long before them, and it will also cause him to be remembered long after their names have vanished from the literary landscape. It concerns MacDonald not as a novelist or writer but as a theologian and teacher of spiritual truth.

MacDonald was a man on a mission, not merely to tell stories but to communicate truth about God and his relationship with man. Trained for the ministry, though MacDonald's first loves lay in the areas of preaching, poetry, and fantasy, after a brief attempted career in the pulpit—cut short when he was essentially ousted for his views—he turned to writing. Following two or three fantasy and poetical works, which were well received but by a very limited audience, in the early 1860s MacDonald began to focus more attention on the novel. The immense popularity of his early attempts soon convinced him that he could convey his deep convictions to a larger audience through fiction than what he had tried before. With but a handful of exceptions, his subsequent stories concern themselves with spiritual themes woven into and through the development of his characters and plots. Thereafter, the novel became his chief form of published work.

Spiritual themes, of course, were well known in the Victorian era, but no other writer of his stature went so far with them or presented life's spiritual side along with the image of an all-loving Father-God with the force and clarity of MacDonald's wisdom and insight. His influence in his day, therefore, was not merely as a novelist but also as a spiritual seer. Queen Victoria presented his *Robert Falconer* to each of her grandchildren, and numerous notables of the day (John Ruskin and Lady Byron as prominent examples) considered him a spiritual mentor and friend.

MacDonald's active writing career spanned most of the last half of the nineteenth century, reaching its height between 1860 and 1890. He eventually wrote more than fifty books, including more than thirty realistic novels, numerous short stories, poems, fantasies, and fairy tales, as well as eight volumes of sermons and literary essays. If the surviving reports from family members and friends are accurate, he was greatly loved by all who knew him. Some ventured to call him a prophet. That he founded no organization, wrote no autobiography, gathered about him no disciples, did not promote himself, emphasized obedience to God as the only and essential meaning to life, and died neither wealthy nor acclaimed by the new century, may go far to validate such appellation.

As time passed, after George MacDonald's death in 1905, not only did literary tastes change, so did spiritual inclinations. The twentieth-century general culture was kind neither to bulky sentences nor to the Christian faith. Men like MacDonald faded from public view. The difficulty was exacerbated by the fact that MacDonald's profound (and perhaps prophetic) spiritual perspectives were embedded in books and presented in a wordy and complex Victorian writing style that gradually became very difficult for the average reader to understand.

MacDonald's reputation was kept from vanishing altogether by the efforts of a few men and women through the years. Not that it probably would have vanished entirely. There were sufficient copies of his books in circulation in both Great Britain and the U.S. (figures are unknown, but they almost surely numbered in the multiple millions) that many continued to discover his works on dusty shelves, in attics, in old bookstores—often not realizing what they were in for until being unexpectedly moved by his powerful insights. In addition, a few important public efforts kept MacDonald's work in view.

The first and probably most significant of these came from two of MacDonald's sons. Both were devoted not only to the memory of their father but also to keeping his work, reputation, and spiritual vision alive so that it could influence future generations. Both became successful authors in their own right, and both wrote biographies that placed MacDonald's life and work in historical perspective and assured that its impact would not be forgotten. Without their efforts, much about their father's life would surely by now have been lost.

The first, *George MacDonald: A Personal Note*, by Ranald MacDonald, formed chapter three of the book *From a Northern Window*, a volume of essays on Scottish topics by nine Scottish authors (London: James Nisbet & Co., 1911). This is more accurately a memorial sketch rather than a biography, yet it is both touching and valuable in its very human portrayal of MacDonald.

The second, *George MacDonald and His Wife*, by eldest son, Greville MacDonald (London: George Allen & Unwin, Ltd. 1924), stands at the other end of the spectrum as a towering biographical work of more than five hundred pages. Released in 1924, along with several other new special editions of MacDonald's books, to commemorate the centennial of his birth, it provides the foundation for much of what is today known of MacDonald's life. Another important volume published at this time, John Malcolm Bulloch's *A Centennial Bibliography of George MacDonald*, presented the first full cataloging of the many editions of MacDonald's life work.

One of the most notable features of Greville MacDonald's biography, in particular, is its introduction by G. K. Chesterton (critic, essayist, humorist, artist, novelist, Christian apologist, and journalist), whose reputation in England at the time had risen to its height. Chesterton's praise for MacDonald's work, as well as his appreciation for its impact upon him personally, could not be ignored. It ensured that a whole new generation—especially in London's literary circles, where Chesterton was a towering figure—heard about the man who had been born a hundred years before in northern Scotland. Chesterton had written MacDonald's obituary in the London *Daily News* in 1905, calling him "one of the three or four greatest men of the nineteenth century." Now, nineteen years later, MacDonald's son called upon him to introduce his dad's biography.

In that introduction, Chesterton spoke of his delight upon first discovering MacDonald's fairy tales and the new world they opened to him. His experience seems to be universal. As all MacDonald readers find, each discovers his or her own magical entrance into George MacDonald's world in a uniquely personal way. For Chesterton, the door happened to be *The Princess and the Goblin*. For many, *At the Back of the North Wind* causes a similar birth of wonder in the soul. For me, the doorway opened through the realistic novels *Sir Gibbie* and *Malcolm*, which produced an explosion of light in my heart and brain. It is surely testimony to MacDonald's versatility that multiple genres are able to beget similar effects on the spiritual imagination of his readers.

MacDonald himself writes about this process of slipping into magical literary worlds, little realizing to what extent his own writing would produce just that effect in countless readers in the decades, and even centuries to come. Indeed, seven magical doors into a world of talking beasts would become notable literary moments of magic for millions a century later, not through MacDonald's own pen, but from that of his most famous literary protégé, C. S. Lewis.

In his very first full-length book, *Phantastes*, which he called "A Faerie Romance for Men and Women," published in 1858, MacDonald leads his readers through the first of many such moments of transitional magic, in this case into the land of Faerie.

> I awoke one morning, [the book's narrator begins,] with the usual perplexity of mind which accompanies the return of consciousness. As I lay and looked through the eastern window of my room, a faint streak of peach-colour, dividing a cloud that just rose above the low swell of the horizon, announced the approach of the sun. As my

thoughts, which a deep and apparently dreamless sleep had dissolved, began again to assume crystalline forms, the strange events of the foregoing night presented themselves anew to my wondering consciousness. . . .

While these strange events were passing through my mind, I suddenly, as one awakes to the consciousness that the sea has been moaning by him for hours, or that the storm has been howling about his window all night, became aware of the sound of running water near me; and looking out of bed, I saw that a large green marble basin, in which I was wont to wash, and which stood on a low pedestal of the same material in a corner of my room, was overflowing like a spring; and that a stream of clear water was running over the carpet, all the length of the room, finding its outlet I knew not where. And, stranger still, where this carpet, which I had myself designed to imitate a field of grass and daisies, bordered the course of the little stream, the grass-blades and daises seemed to wave in a tiny breeze that followed the water's flow; while under the rivulet they bent and swayed with every motion of the changeful current, as if they were about to dissolve with it, and, forsaking their fixed form, become fluent as the waters.

My dressing-table was an old-fashioned piece of furniture of black oak, with drawers all down the front. These were elaborately carved in foliage, of which ivy formed the chief part. The nearer end of this table remained just as it had been, but on the further end a singular change had commenced. I happened to fix my eye on a little cluster of ivy leaves. The first of these was evidently the work of the carver; the next looked curious; the third was unmistakably ivy; and just beyond it a tendril of clematis had twined itself about the gilt handle of one of the drawers. Hearing next a slight motion above me, I looked up, and saw that the branches and leaves designed upon the curtains of my bed were slightly in motion. Not knowing what change might follow next, I thought it high time to get up; and, springing from the bed, my bare feet alighted upon a cool green sward; and although I dressed in all haste, I found myself completing my toilet under the boughs of a great tree, whose top waved in the golden stream of the sunrise with many interchanging lights, and with shadows of leaf and branch gliding over leaf and branch, as the cool morning wind swung it to and fro, like a sinking sea-wave.

When the second chapter of *Lilith* is placed alongside the above passage from *Phantastes*—"I had been looking at rather than into the mirror, when suddenly I became aware that it reflected neither the chamber nor my own person. I have an impression of having seen the wall melt away. . . . I saw before me a wild country, broken and heathy. Desolate hills of no great height . . . occupied the middle distance. . . . Nearest me lay a tract of moorland, flat and melancholy"—can any insightful reader doubt that when MacDonald penned the opening scenes of these two books, Narnia was born?

Indeed, it was *Phantastes*, by producing such magical

entry into George MacDonald's world through fairyland, that would lead to the most significant elevation of its author's reputation in the twentieth century. In 1916, the curious title caught the eye of a seventeen-year-old atheist at the bookstall of a train station outside London. The impact was immediate, though the result took years to reach fruition. The young man's name was Clive Staples Lewis. Thirteen years later, when he, as he says, reluctantly accepted the Christian faith, it was to MacDonald he pointed as the man who had set his feet in that direction.

Years later Lewis wrote:

> It must be more than thirty years ago that I bought—almost unwillingly, for I had looked at the volume on that bookstall and rejected it on a dozen previous occasions—the Everyman edition of *Phantastes*. A few hours later I knew that I had crossed a great frontier. . . . What it actually did to me was to convert, even to baptize . . . my imagination. It did nothing to my intellect nor (at that time) to my conscience. Their turn came far later and with the help of many other books and men. But when the process was complete—by which, of course, I mean "when it had *really* begun"—I found that I was still with MacDonald and that he had accompanied me all the way and that I was now at last ready to hear from him much that he could not have told me at that first meeting. But in a sense, what he was now telling me was the very same that he had told me from the beginning. (From the Introduction, C. S. Lewis, *George MacDonald: An Anthology*, 1946)

As Lewis went on to worldwide fame as a Christian spokesman and apologist, he always considered MacDonald his literary spiritual mentor and a completely unique figure in his life.

Throughout a lifetime of correspondence, mention of MacDonald frequently pops up in Lewis's letters. MacDonald appears as a central character in Lewis's *The Great Divorce*. Lewis quotes MacDonald several times in *Mere Christianity*. And MacDonald, of course, occupies a central role in Lewis's conversion as recounted in *Surprised by Joy*.

Yet all his life Lewis remained frustrated that the notoriety of his own books continued to grow, while his readership seemed to take little notice of MacDonald, not only as the foundation stone of his faith but also of his theological perspective and spiritual outlook. Lewis wrote,

> I have never concealed the fact that I regarded him as my master; indeed I fancy I have never written a book in which I did not quote from him. But it has not seemed to me that those who have received my books kindly take even now sufficient notice of the affiliation. Honesty drives me to emphasize it. (*George MacDonald: An Anthology*, 20)

This frustration, and the "honesty" that compelled him, led Lewis in 1946 to release a short volume of collected quotations from George MacDonald, *George MacDonald: An Anthology*, taken mostly from the three volumes entitled *Unspoken Sermons*. In the lengthy introduction to his anthology, Lewis presented a biographical sketch of MacDonald's life, emphasizing—as every biographer of necessity must—those aspects of MacDonald's life, work, and thought that were most meaningful to him and that had contributed to his own pilgrimage from atheism to Christianity.

Though his anthology introduced a few individuals to MacDonald's ideas in the years that followed, the impact remained modest. By the late 1960s, not a single of MacDonald's novels, not one of his sermons or poems or literary essays, were in print. Of his more than fifty books, only two fairy tales, the two adult fantasies, *Phantastes* and *Lilith*, and a handful of short stories remained obtainable.

It is not that MacDonald was in danger of being lost sight of; Lewis's increasing popularity ensured that an expanding nucleus of his readership was slowly drawn into an appreciation for MacDonald on the basis of the association between the two men. But the *availability* of his work was disappearing. The two most important genres of his lifetime corpus—his novels and spiritual writings—were simply unavailable. Though his name circulated in select literary circles (W. H. Auden wrote the introduction to a new edition of *Phantastes* and *Lilith* in 1954, in which he called MacDonald "one of the most remarkable writers of the nineteenth century"), for most people his books were not to be had.

In 1965, two years after Lewis's death, Dr. Clyde Kilby, professor of English at Wheaton College outside Chicago—himself a devoted Lewis admirer who had done his best through the years to inform his students and others of the Lewis-MacDonald connection, and who had just completed one of the first full-length studies of Lewis, *The Christian World of C. S. Lewis*—conceived the idea of establishing a memorial collection of books, manuscripts, and other materials associated with Lewis. Along with those of his favorite author, Kilby decided to include the works of six other writers in his collection, each of whom either knew Lewis or was in some way associated with his legacy. No doubt recognizing the need to preserve the dwindling availability of MacDonald volumes, MacDonald headed this list, along with G. K. Chesterton, Dorothy Sayers, and Lewis's three fellow Oxford "Inklings"—J. R. R. Tolkien, Charles Williams, and Owen Barfield. Kilby named the collection after its benefactor, Marion E. Wade, and the Wade Center at Wheaton College grew to become the primary library and research center for the study of and preservation of the works of its seven authors.

Recognition of MacDonald's importance continued slowly and almost invisibly to spread in small academic and literary circles. An increasing number of graduate studies and critical works began to appear during the 1970s. A major volume of essays dedicated and presented to Clyde Kilby (*Imagination and the Spirit*, Charles Huttar, ed.) was published in 1971, which included an essay on MacDonald by Wheaton graduate Dr. Glenn Sadler. Richard Reis's excellent book *George MacDonald* appeared in 1972. A significant two-volume edition of MacDonald's stories was published by Eerdmans in 1973 with an informative introduction by Dr. Sadler. Yet though MacDonald's name was slowly coming to be recognized in the scholarly circles associated with Wheaton College, these efforts accomplished little to make his full corpus *available* in a widespread way.

As I look back from the present to those years, I find myself echoing Lewis's words: "It must be more than thirty years ago"—when I first discovered George MacDonald in 1971. As with many, the name *MacDonald* came to my own attention first through Lewis, whose *Mere Christianity*, *The Great Divorce*, and *The Chronicles of Narnia* I had recently discovered. I still had no idea to what an extent Lewis's ideas had their roots in MacDonald's volume of work, nor to what an extent the foundations for Narnia could be observed in *Phantastes*, *Lilith*, and MacDonald's two *Curdie* books. All I knew was that if MacDonald represented more of what I had found so delightful in Lewis, then I wanted to know of it. I was not yet in search of spiritual foundations, only good reading. Fortunately, as I would discover soon enough, the two were one and the same.

At about the same time, a copy of the 1963 edition of *Sir Gibbie*, wonderfully edited by authoress Elizabeth Yates (1905–2001), whetted my appetite still more. It was not her first publication of MacDonald's work: Yates, a close friend of MacDonald's daughter Winifred Louisa Troup, had compiled a volume of his poetry, *Gathered Grace*, which appeared in 1936. Twenty-five years later, dismayed at the growing scarcity of MacDonald's books and the fading of his reputation, she decided to present a newly formatted novel to one of her publishers.

Wee Gibbie's story captivated me—as it had Yates—in a way that surpassed even what I had read in Lewis. Yates' skillfully edited volume drew me into Gibbie's magical world as surely as had my passage through the wardrobe into Narnia a year earlier. Thus began a quest to locate more of the nearly inaccessible works of this nearly forgotten Victorian, beyond the few fantasy and fairy-tale offerings then being published.

Within two or three years, my wife and I managed to obtain most of MacDonald's novels in hundred-year-old editions through antiquarian bookshops. But it wasn't enough to have them for ourselves. I did not find the idea satisfying merely to "collect and preserve" his books as the Wade Center was doing—as important and necessary as that was. I wanted to *share* them. I wanted *everyone* to have the opportunity to know in MacDonald the wonders that many before us, and now we ourselves, had been fortunate enough to discover. It therefore became my personal passion to find some means to reinvigorate *widespread* public interest in George MacDonald.

Sharing the belief of many in MacDonald's singular stature as a Christian thinker, I was convinced that in the right format, and through a new publication forum, MacDonald's writings could speak again to new generations as they had in his own time. It was not enough for him to be known to scattered dozens or hundreds who might chance to hear of him or who had access to rare book editions growing scarcer every year. It wasn't enough for MacDonald to be studied in graduate classes and discussed in symposiums and quoted in books, if the people reading those books and listening to those discussions had no access to those works. My vision was for an availability that would allow *anyone* to obtain copies of MacDonald's writings so that they could underline them and reread them and loan them to friends and give away as many copies as they wanted. My vision was for his books to be *circulated* rather than hoarded, *read* rather than simply cited. And Elizabeth Yates' edition of *Sir Gibbie* gave me a germinal idea as to how such a thing might be possible, along with what I hoped would be a new line of MacDonald originals. Thus began my own work of editing and redacting MacDonald's novels in the Yates tradition—in conjunction with the publication of new editions of the same titles in their full-length formats—hopeful that both efforts might exercise a broad and life-changing influence in many lives and again elevate MacDonald to his rightful stature.

About the same time, in the mid-to-late 1970s, Kilby's colleague at Wheaton, Dr. Rolland Hein, began publishing a small collection of excerpts from MacDonald's work—one from the novels, three books of extracts from the sermons. My own editions—both edited and originals—began to appear soon after, in the early 1980s, which led in 1987 to my biography of MacDonald, *George MacDonald, Scotland's Beloved Storyteller*. Many other editions of MacDonald's books (edited and originals) followed in the next decade from a variety of publishers. Several additional biographies appeared, as well as a number of anthologies and collections. Hein and Sadler added important contributions to the expanding list of titles about MacDonald. Led by Bethany House, whose commitment and variety of MacDonald editions has led the way, the individuals and other publishers involved in this "availability explosion" of his corpus are too numerous to mention, but surely all who love MacDonald owe them a debt of gratitude.

Now, in the early years of the twenty-first century, MacDonald's novels, fairy tales, and stories are thankfully once again obtainable in a widespread way in a great variety of editions and are indeed, as I had foreseen, accessible to all.

Yet that for which his significance is perhaps greatest—particularly considering its impact in the life of C. S. Lewis—MacDonald's *theological nonfiction* remains even now in relative obscurity. Considered by many the most influential Christian writer of the twentieth century, Lewis's books annually sell the world over in the millions. Yet the spiritual and imaginative foundation of those writings remains largely unknown to the vast majority of devoted Lewis readers. Despite Lewis's laudatory words about MacDonald, the wider public has not yet recognized the roots of Lewis's beliefs, nor the degree to which the inspiration for his content came straight from his mentor. MacDonald's nonfiction writings are still not widely available. Lewis's words, more than a half century later, might well have been written today: "It has not seemed to me that those who have received my books kindly take even now sufficient notice of the affiliation."

Hoping at last to address this need, and as part of a centenary remembrance of his death in 1905, I am pleased to inaugurate this new series of nonfiction writings from the pen of George MacDonald. The books in this series are taken from his spoken and written sermons and from selected published essays.

The editing of these selections is as minimal as I have been able to make it. However, extracting the ore from MacDonald's writings does require some effort. I recognize that there will always be those who take exception to the idea of "editing" another's work at all, preferring, one must suppose—so long as such critics have their *own* prized copies to enjoy—that it remain untampered with in the vaults of obscurity rather than be made more generally accessible in a more readable format.

Against such a potential critique I will not reply. Because the fact is, MacDonald's originals are cumbersome to wade through, and that seems to me justification enough. There may be some who do not find them so, but I am not one of them. I find them difficult. Thus my goal is to make MacDonald's wisdom and prophetic insight about God readable and graspable to anyone willing to put in the effort to understand his groundbreaking, unorthodox, and sometimes revolutionary ideas. It is my hope that the minimal editing I have employed with these writings will help you discover these rich veins within MacDonald's thought.

This is not to say, even now, that this will be a light read. MacDonald's ideas and processes of thought are occasionally so profound that nothing makes them easy. We are not used to having to think quite so strenuously for our spiritual food. We live in a superficial age where doctrinal formula provides the parameters by which spirituality is judged.

MacDonald saw things differently. Doctrinal formula was nothing to him. His unique perspective takes some getting used to. I find that many passages require two or three readings. But I also find spiritual gold awaiting me, sometimes buried deep but always ready to shine out brilliantly from the page when suddenly I *see* it. Theologically, too, as imaginatively, I have discovered many doors of delight opening before me into new worlds of wonder about God and his work. In my life at least, I have found these nonfiction writings just as "magical" and full of wonder as *Malcolm* and *Narnia*.

I am aware that it is a high and holy calling to try to recast the words of another into a form that truly represents his intent. It is with prayerful trepidation that I undertake such a task with MacDonald's spiritual writings. When editing his novels twenty years ago, my task was distinct from this. I was forced by the constraints of publication to shorten the originals. In many cases, because of the language employed, it was also necessary to "translate" portions from the Scot's dialect of the originals.

With MacDonald's nonfiction, the case is different. There is no dialect. No need exists to shorten. Therefore, except for a few rare words and perhaps a very occasional phrase, I have removed little. What I have done, rather, is simply to shorten sentences and paragraphs, that I might order MacDonald's progression of thought in a more linear and straightforward fashion than is sometimes presented in the originals.

Some will wonder why such editing is necessary. For two reasons: because of the complex progression of MacDonald's ideas, and because of the elaborately entangled grammatical constructions in which he expressed these ideas.

I would not presume to call MacDonald's logic other than straightforward. The operation of his mind is so far above mine that I would dare no such presumption. I think I am on safe ground to say, however, that as his logic progresses it brings in its train multitudinous tangential modifiers and explanations and offshoot points so that it often becomes very difficult to follow the primary sequence of ideas. Once or twice a page, it seems,

I have to stop to read a lengthy section four or five times simply to "get it."

Additionally, MacDonald's grammar and syntax can become extremely involved and can impede understanding. Sentences of one hundred to one hundred twenty words are common, occasionally reaching one hundred sixty or one hundred eighty. These often contain half a dozen semicolons, several dashes, numerous commas, and a colon or two. He can use *every* punctuation mark in a single sentence! Likewise, his paragraphs are extremely long and can run to five or six pages.

For the most part, MacDonald's ideas are here expressed in the words in which he wrote them, or, if some change has been necessary, in something very close to them. Where his originals are straightforward and clear, they are reproduced without change. Where the word-thickets are complicated and the sentences long, structural editing has been done but most of his actual *words* kept intact.

Clarity sometimes requires brevity. We live in a time when we are not adept at working our way through theologically dense sentences. Simplifying the complexity of the originals in these two areas— thought progressions and grammatical constructions— enables MacDonald's meaning and expressiveness to rise to the surface with more radiance. Breaking up thought progressions into smaller chunks is an enormous aid to understanding.

One of the chapters contained a mere eighteen paragraphs. As I have rendered it, it now contains approximately seventy. I am confident you will find, as I do, that the ideas are easier to grasp with a little more white space on the page. Most of what I have done, therefore, is more structural than editorial. Clarity, not brevity, has been the goal.

Finally, the subheadings within the text are my own additions, again, provided as an aid to comprehension without materially altering the text.

An example or two may help illustrate this structural complexity I have tried to address.

The following one hundred forty word sentence appears in the original of "The Creation in Christ":

> I worship the Son as the human God the divine, the only Man, deriving his being and power from the Father, equal with him as a son is the equal at once and the subject of his father—but making himself the equal of his father in what is most precious in Godhead, namely Love—which is indeed, the essence of that statement of the evangelist with which I have now to do—a higher thing than the making of the worlds and the things in them, which he did by the power of the Father, not by a self-existent power in himself, whence the apostle, to whom the Lord must have said things he did not say to the rest, or who was better able to receive what he said to all, says, "All things were made" not by, but "through him."

Obviously we can "understand" MacDonald's words—this is nothing like the Scottish dialect of his novels. But it takes a little mental work to unsnarl the complexity of the construction.

Another sentence of two hundred eighteen words

comes to us with three semicolons, five dashes, and twenty-four commas:

> *But I will ask whether to know better and do not so well, is not a serving of Satan;—whether to lead men on in the name of God as towards the best when the end is not the best, is not a serving of Satan;—whether to flatter their pride by making them conquerors of the enemies of their nation instead of their own evils, is not a serving of Satan; —in a word, whether, to desert the mission of God, who knew that men could not be set free in that way, and sent him to be a man, a true man, the one man, among them, that his life might become their life, and that so they might be as free in prison or on the cross, as upon a hill-side or on a throne,— whether, so deserting the truth, to give men over to the lie of believing other than spirit and truth to be the worship of the Father, other than love the fulfilling of the law, other than the offering of their best selves the service of God, other than obedient harmony with the primal love and truth and law, freedom,—whether, to desert God thus, and give men over thus, would not have been to fall down and worship the devil.*

Both examples, it should be pointed out, are embedded in the midst of paragraphs of even greater length. Therefore, if MacDonald's meaning can be preserved, even enhanced, by reducing sentence length and presenting his ideas in a more "straight line," it only makes sense to do so.

In addition, we must remember that these selections

were all written more than a century ago. Methods of communication have changed. Words themselves have changed. For the sake of clarity, where denotations (literal meanings) and connotations (implied meanings) have shifted, some of these issues have also been addressed. In one of these selections I encountered the word *car*, though MacDonald's writing preceded the invention of the automobile by a decade or two. I felt that this particular word's use in the text, now in 2005, obscured the meaning. After a brief sojourn through a nineteenth-century dictionary, ten minutes of reflection, and various attempts to render the passage with slight difference, I arrived at what I felt satisfied MacDonald's meaning. Likewise, I have replaced *simulacrum, penetralia, Hyperion, palimpsest, adytum, simper,* and the like. Of course, such words can be looked up in a dictionary, but how many would stop to do so?

Even after all this, MacDonald's language may still sound somewhat laborious to some. While untangling lengthy sentences and paragraphs into more straightforward progressions, I have yet tried to retain the essential character and flavor of his modes of expression; some of what follows, therefore, may still be hard going. In "The Creation in Christ" MacDonald probes the depths of the very Godhead itself. This isn't a self-help or experiential treatise in "Christianity Lite" but theology at its most profound.

Yet here we discover the spiritual foundation of C. S. Lewis's faith. Should we therefore expect anything less than a theology worthy of his great mind? I invite you to discover why Lewis wrote,

My own debt to this book [the three volumes of *Unspoken Sermons*] is almost as great as one man can owe to another: and nearly all serious inquirers to whom I have introduced it acknowledge that it has given them great help—sometimes indispensable help towards the very acceptance of the Christian faith.

It seems only fitting, in preparing us at last to move on to MacDonald himself, that we listen again to Lewis as he describes what made these writings so unique and powerful in his own development:

> In MacDonald it is always the voice of conscience that speaks. He addresses the will: the demand for obedience, for "something to be neither more nor less nor other than *done*," is incessant. . . . The Divine Sonship is the key-conception which unites all the different elements of his thought. I dare not say that he is never in error; but to speak plainly I know hardly any other writer who seems to be closer, or more continually close, to the Spirit of Christ himself. Hence his Christ-like union of tenderness and severity. Nowhere else outside the New Testament have I found terror and comfort so intertwined. . . . All the sermons are suffused with a spirit of love and wonder. (*George MacDonald: An Anthology*, 18–20)

Michael Phillips
Eureka, California

*All things were made by him, and
without him was not anything made that
was made. In him was life, and the life
was the light of men.*

—JOHN 1:3–4

The Creation
in Christ

GEORGE MACDONALD

— A DIFFICULTY —

It seems to me that any thinking lover of the gospel, and especially one accustomed to the effort of communicating ideas with clarity, can hardly have failed to feel something of a dissatisfaction with the close of the third verse of the opening chapter of John's gospel as the Authorized Version presents it to English readers. It seems to me, in its feebleness, unlike and rhetorically unworthy of the rest.

Perhaps it is no worse than redundant, and therefore unnecessary. But that is no satisfaction to the man who would find, if possible, perfection in the words of the beloved disciple who was nearer the Lord than any other. The phrase *that was made* seems, from its uselessness, weak even to foolishness after what precedes it: "All things were made by him, and without him was not anything made that was made."

My hope was great, therefore, when in reading the Greek I saw that the shifting of a period would rid me of the surplus words. If by such a change any precious result of meaning should follow, the change would not merely be justifiable—seeing that mere points of ink on ancient texts are of no authority with anyone accustomed to the vagaries of scribes, editors, and printers—but one for which to give thanks to God.

Indeed, I found the change unfolded such a truth as to show the rhetoric itself in accordance with the highest thought of the apostle. I was so glad of the sudden new meaning that it added little to my satisfaction to discover the change actually was supported by the best original manuscripts and versions. Furthermore, I learned that the passage had been a cause of much disputation in light of the two possible renditions. And the ground of argument on the side of the common reading of 1611 seemed to me worse than worthless.

— WONDERFUL NEW LIGHT —

Let us then look at the passage as I think it ought to be translated. Then let us seek the meaning for the sake of which it was written. This meaning is by no means solely dependent for its revelation on this single passage. Indeed, its truth belongs to the very truth as it exists in Jesus. But if I am right in the interpretation which suggested itself the moment I saw the probable rhetorical relation of the words, then we find that truth magnificently expressed here by the apostle, and differently from anywhere else.

I will now set down the passage recast into two sentences distinct from the above, with the separating period differently placed:

"All things were made through him, and without him was made not one thing. That which was made in him was life, and the life was the light of men."

Note the antithesis of the *through* and the *in:*

"All things were made *through* him. . . . That which was made *in* him . . ."

In this grand assertion seems to me to lie, more than merely shadowed, the germ of creation and redemption—of all the divine in its relation to all the human.

— AN ETERNAL FATHER AND AN ETERNAL SON —

In attempting to set forth what I find in it, I write with no desire to provoke controversy, which I loathe, but with some hope of presenting to the minds of those capable of seeing it the glory of the truth of the Father and the Son as spoken by this first of seers in the grand fashion of his insight. I am as indifferent to a reputation for orthodoxy as I despise the championship of novelty. To the untrue, the truth itself must seem unsound, for the light that is in them is darkness.

I believe, then, that Jesus Christ is the eternal Son of the eternal Father. I believe that from the first beginnings of all things Jesus is the Son, because God is the Father. This statement is imperfect and unfit because it is an attempt of human thought to represent that which it cannot grasp, yet which it believes so strongly that it must try to utter it even in speech that cannot be right.

I believe therefore that the Father is the greater, and that if the Father had not been, the Son could not have been.

I will apply no logic to this thesis, nor would I even now state the above but for the sake of what is to follow. The true heart will remember the inadequacy of our speech, and our thought also, when it turns to the things that lie near the unknown roots of our existence. In saying what I do, I only say what Paul implies when he speaks of the Lord giving up the kingdom to his Father that God may be all in all.

I worship the Son as the human God, the divine, the only perfect Man. He derives his being and power from the Father, and is equal with him as a son is both the equal and at the same time the subject of his father. *Yet he makes himself the equal of his Father only in what is most precious in the Godhead, namely, Love.* This is indeed the essence of that statement of John the evangelist, which I am now considering. It is a higher thing than the making of the worlds and the things in them, which making he did by the power of the Father, not by a self-existent power in himself. For this reason, the apostle, to whom the Lord must have said things he did not say to the rest, or who was better able to receive what he said to them all—says, "All things were made" not *by,* but *"through* him."

We must not wonder things away into nonentity, but try to present them to ourselves after what fashion we are able—even though these attempts will be but shadows of full heavenly truth. For our very beings and understandings and consciousnesses, though but shadows in regard to any perfection either of outline or operation, are yet shadows of *his* being, *his* understanding, *his* consciousness. He has cast those shadows. They are no more originally our own than his power of creation is ours.

— A TWOFOLD CREATION —

In our shadow-speech, then, following with my shadow-understanding as best I can the words of the evangelist, I say:

The Father, in bringing out of the unseen the things that are seen, made essential use of the Son. All that exists, therefore, was created *through* him. What may be the difference between the part in creation of the Father and the part of the Son, who can understand? Perhaps we may one day come to see into it a little. For I dare hope that, through our own willed sonship, we too shall come far nearer ourselves to creating. The word *creation* applied to the loftiest success of human genius seems to me a mockery of a humanity which is in itself still in the process of creation.

Let us read the text again.

"All things were made *through* him, and without him was made not one thing. That which was made *in* him was life."

Do you begin to see it? The power by which he created the worlds was given him by his father. But he had in himself a yet greater power than this. Something *else* was made, not *through* but *in* him. He brought something into being *by himself*, not by virtue of the Father working through him. In this other thing he creates in his own grand way—self-generated from within his own being—as did the Father. And John tells us exactly what this other thing was.

"That which was made *in* him was *life*."

What does this mean? What is the *life* the apostle is speaking of? Many forms of life have come to being *through* the Son. But those are results, not forms of the life that was brought to existence *in* him. He could not have been employed by the Father in creating except in virtue of the life that was *in* him.

— THE GREAT MYSTERY OF GOD'S EXISTENCE —

As to what the life of God is to himself, all we can know is that we cannot know it. Even that, however, is not absolute ignorance. For no one can see that, from its very nature, he cannot understand a thing without therein approaching that thing in a genuine manner. As to what the life of God is in relation to us, we know that it is the causing life of everything that we call life—of everything that is. In knowing this, we know something of that life by the very forms of its force.

But there are two great mysteries that lie absolutely beyond us. I presume that, in fact, the two actually make but one mystery. It is a mystery that must be a mystery to us for ever, not because God will not explain it, but because God himself could not make us understand it if he tried to explain it.

The one interminable mystery is, first, how he can be self-existent, and next, how he can make other beings exist. Self-existence and creation no man will ever understand.

Again, regarding the matter from the side of the creature—the cause of his being precedes that being. He can therefore have no knowledge of his own creation. Neither could he understand that which he can do nothing like. If we could make ourselves, we should understand our creation, but to do that we must be God. And this, of all ideas, seems to me the most dismal and hopeless—that I, with the self-dissatisfied and painfully limited consciousness I possess, could in any way have caused myself.

Nevertheless, if I be a child of God, I must be *like* him, like him even in the matter of this creative energy by which we exist but which we cannot understand. There must be something in me that corresponds in its childish way to the eternal power in him.

But I am forestalling.

— THE DEEPEST IN GOD —

The question now is: What was that life, the thing made *in* the Son—made by him inside himself, not outside him—made not *through* but *in* him—the life that was his own, as God's is his own?

It was, I answer, that act in him that corresponded in him, as the Son, to the self-existence of his father.

Now, what is the deepest in God . . . his power?

No, for power could not make him what we mean when we say *God*. As powerful as it might be, evil could, of course, never create one atom. But let us understand very plainly that a being whose essence was only power would be such a negation of the divine that no righteous worship could be offered him. It would be possible only to fear him. Such a being, even if he were righteous in judgment, yet could not be God. The God himself whom we love could not be righteous were he not something deeper and better still than we generally mean by the word. But alas, how little can language say without seeming to say something wrong!

In one word, God is *Love*.

Love is the deepest depth, the essence of his nature. Love is at the root of all his being. It is not merely that he could not be God if he had made no creatures to whom to be God. But love is the heart and hand of his creation. It is his right to create, and his power to create as well. The love that foresees creation is itself the power to create. Neither could he be righteous—that is, fair to his creatures—but that his love created them. His perfection is his love. All his divine rights rest upon his love.

Ah, he is not the great monarch! The simplest peasant loving his cow is more divine than any monarch whose monarchy is his glory. If God would not punish sin, or if he did it for anything but love, he would not be the father of Jesus Christ, the God who works as Jesus works.

What then, I ask again, is in Christ correspondent to the creative power of God? It must be something that comes also of love. And in the Son the love must express itself to that which already exists, namely, God. Because of that eternal love which has no beginning, the Father must have the Son. God could not love, could not be love, without making things to love: Jesus has God to love. The love of the Son is responsive to the love of the Father.

— THE LIFE IN THE SON —
CHOSEN YIELDING OF WILL

Within the Godhead, then, are two forms of the divine love that point in opposite directions but which reveal that same love: *Creating* love and *self-denying* love.

The response to self-existent love is self-abnegating love. The refusal of himself is that in Jesus which corresponds to the creation of God. His love takes action, creates, in self-abjuration, in the death of self as motive, in the drowning of self in the life of God, where it lives only as love.

What is life in a child? Is it not perfect response to his parents, thorough oneness with them? A child at strife with his parents, one in whom their will is not his, is no true child. As a *child*—in the way God means the word—he is dead. His death is manifest in rigidity and contortion. His spiritual order is on the way to chaos. Disintegration has begun. Death is at work in him.

See the same child yielding to the will that is righteously above his own, and then see the life begin to flow from the heart through the members. He relaxes and the light rises like a fountain in his eyes and a flash from his face! Life again knows its lordship!

The life of Christ is this—negatively, that he does nothing, cares for nothing for his own sake, and positively, that he cares with his whole soul for the will and pleasure of his father. Because his father is his father, therefore he will be his *child*.

— ETERNAL CHILDNESS, THE ORIGIN OF *LIFE* —

The truth in Jesus is his relation to his father. The righteousness of Jesus is his fulfillment of that relation. Meeting this relation, loving his father with his whole being, he is not merely alive as born of God, but, giving himself with perfect will to God, choosing to die to himself and live to God, he therein creates in himself a new and higher life. Standing upon himself, he has gained the power to awaken life, the divine shadow of his own, in the hearts of us his brothers and sisters. We have come from the same birth-home as himself, namely, the heart of his God and our God, his father and our father. But without our elder brother to do it first, we would never have chosen that self-abjuration which is life, and never have become alive like him.

To will, not from self, but with the Eternal, is to live.

This choice of his own being, in the full knowledge of what he did—this active willing to be the Son of the Father, perfect in *obedience*—is that in Jesus which responds and corresponds to the self-existence of God. Jesus rose at once to the height of his being and set himself down on the throne of his nature in the act of *subjecting* himself to the will of the Father as his only good, the only *reason* of his existence. When he died on the cross, he did—in the wild weather of his outlying provinces and in the torture of the body of his revelation—that which he had done at home in glory and gladness. From the infinite beginning—for here I can speak only by contradictions—he completed and held fast the eternal circle of his existence in saying, *"Thy will, not mine, be done!"*

He made himself what he is by *deathing* himself into the will of the eternal Father, through which will he was the eternal Son—thus plunging into the fountain of his own life, the everlasting Fatherhood, and taking the Godhead of the Son.

This is the life that was made *in* Jesus: "That which was made in him was life."

This life, self-willed in Jesus, is the one thing that

makes such life—the eternal life, the true life—possible, imperative, essential, to every man, woman, and child. The Father has sent us all into this outer world that we may go back into the inner world of his own heart. As the self-existent life of the Father has given us *being*, so the willed devotion of Jesus is his power to give us *eternal life* like his own—to enable us to do the same. There is no life for any man other than the same kind that Jesus has. His disciple must live by the same absolute devotion of his will to the Father's. Then is the life of the disciple one with the life of the Father.

— JESUS, THE FATHER OF OUR CHILDSHIP —

Because we are come out of the divine nature, which chooses to be divine, we also must *choose* to be divine. We must choose to be of God, to be one with God. We must choose to love and live as he loves and lives. We must choose to be partakers of the divine nature or we perish.

Man cannot originate this life. It must be shown him, and he must choose it. God is the father of Jesus and of us—of every possibility of our being. But while God is the father of his children, Jesus is the father of their childship. For in him is made the life which is sonship to the Father—namely, the recognition, in fact and life, that the Father has his claim upon his sons and daughters.

We are not and cannot become true sons without our will willing his will. Our doing follows his making. It was the will of Jesus to be what God willed and meant him to be that made him the true Son of God. He was not the Son of God because he could not help it, but because he willed to be in himself the Son that he was in the divine idea.

So with us: We must *be* the sons and daughters we are. We are not made to be what we cannot help being. True sons and daughters do not exist after such fashion! We are sons and daughters in God's claim. Then we must *be* sons and daughters in our will.

And we can be sons and daughters, saved into the original necessity and bliss of our being, only by choosing God for the Father he is and doing his will—yielding ourselves as true sons to the absolute Father. Therein lies the only and essential human bliss. The working out of this our salvation must be pain, and the handing of it down to them that are below must ever be in pain. Even so, the eternal form of the will of God in and for us is intensity of bliss.

— LIGHT: A REVELATION OF LIFE —

"And the life was the light of men."

The life of which I have been speaking became light to men in the appearing of him in whom it came into being. The *life* became *light* that men might see it. Seeing it, they themselves might live by choosing that life also, by choosing so to live and to be.

There is always something deeper than anything we can say—something of which all human words, figures, and pictures are but the outer overlaying spheres through which the central reality from within shines more or less plainly. Light itself is but the poor outside form of a deeper, better thing—namely, *life*.

The life is Christ. The light too is Christ, but only the body of Christ. The life is Christ himself. The light is what we *see* and shall see in him. The life is what we may *be* in him. The life "is a light by abundant clarity invisible." It is the unspeakable unknown. It must become light such as men can *see* before men can *know* it.

Therefore, the obedient human God appeared as the obedient divine man, doing the works of his father—that is, the things which his father did—doing them humbly before unfriendly brethren. The Son of the Father must take his own form in the substance of flesh, that he may be seen of men and so become the *light* of men—not that men may have light, but that men may have *life*. Seeing what they could not originate, they may, through the life that is in them, begin to hunger after the life of which they are capable and which is essential to their being.

In the same way that root and stem may thirst for the flower for whose sake, and through whose presence in them they exist, so too may the life in men cause them to long for him who is their life and thirst for its own perfection within them. That the child of God may become the son of God by beholding *the* Son, his life is revealed in light. Thus, the radiant heart of the Son of God is sunlight to his fellows. In order that the idea of what we were made for may be drawn out by the presence and drawing of the Ideal, that Ideal, the perfect Son of the Father, was sent to his brethren.

— THE SON REVEALS THE FATHER IN LIGHT —

Let us not forget that the devotion of the Son could never have been but for the devotion of the Father. The Father never seeks his own glory one atom more than does the Son. He is devoted to the Son, and to all his sons and daughters, with a perfect and eternal devotion and with fathomless unselfishness. The whole being and doing of Jesus on earth is the same as his being and doing from all eternity, that being and doing whereby he is the blessed Son-God of the Father-God. His being and doing on earth is the shining out of that life that men might see it.

It is a *being* like God, a *doing* of the will of God, a working of the works of God. It is an unveiling of the Father in the Son so that men may know him. It is the prayer of the Son for the rest of the sons to come back to the Father, to be reconciled to the Father, to behave to the Father as he does.

Jesus seems to me to say:

> *I know your father, for he is my father. I know him because I have been with him from eternity. You do not know him. I have come to you to tell you that as I am, such is he, to tell you that he is just like me, only greater and better. He only is the true, original good. I am true because I seek nothing but his will. He only is all in all. I am not all in all, but he is my father, and I am the son in whom his heart of love is satisfied.*
>
> *Come home with me and sit with me on the throne of my obedience. Together we will do his will and be glad with him. For his will is the only good.*
>
> *You may do with me as you please. I will not defend myself. Because I speak truly, my witness is unswerving. I stand to it come what may. If I held my face to my testimony only till danger came close, and then prayed for the Father to deliver me with*

twelve legions of angels, that would be to say that the Father would do anything for his children until it began to hurt him. I bear witness that my father is such as I. In the face of death I assert it, and dare death to disprove it. Kill me, do what you will and can against me, my father is true, and I am true in saying that he is true. Danger or hurt cannot turn me aside from this my witness. Death can only kill my body but cannot make me its captive.

Father, thy will be done! The pain will pass. It will be but for a time! Gladly will I suffer that men may know that I live, and that thou art my life. Be with me, Father, that it may not be more than I can bear.

Friends, if you think anything less than this could redeem the world, or make blessed any child that God has created, you know neither the Son nor the Father.

— THE BOND OF THE UNIVERSE —

The bond of the universe, the chain that holds it together, the one active unity, the harmony of things, the uniting of difference, the reconciliation of all external appearances and wandering desires and returning loves is the devotion of the Son to the Father. This devotion is the fact at the root of every vision which reveals that "love is the only good in the world," and selfishness the one thing hateful in the city of the living God. It is the life of the universe.

It is not the fact that God created all things that makes the universe a whole. It is rather that he through whom he created them loves him perfectly and is eternally content in his father and satisfied to be because his father is with him. It is not the fact that God is all in all that unites the universe. Rather it is the love of the Son to the Father. Of no onehood comes unity—there can be no oneness where there is only one. For the very beginnings of unity there must be two. Without Christ, therefore, there could be no universe.

The reconciliation wrought by Jesus is not the primary source of unity in the world. That reconciliation was the necessary working out of the prior eternal fact, which made that fact potent upon the rest of the family. The eternal fact is that God and Christ are one. They are Father and Son. The Father loves the Son as only the Father can love. The Son loves the Father as only the Son can love.

The prayer of the Lord for unity between men and the Father and himself springs from the eternal need of love. The more I regard it, the more I am lost in the wonder and glory of the thing. Were it not for the Father and the Son, no two humans on earth would care a jot for each other. It might be the right way for creatures to love because of mere existence, but what two creatures would ever have originated the loving? I cannot for a moment believe it would have been. Even had I come into being as I am now with an inclination to love, selfishness would soon have overpowered it.

But if the Father loves the Son, if the very music that makes the harmony of life lies not in the theory of love in the heart of the Father but in the fact of it, in the burning love in the hearts of Father and Son, then glory be to the Father and to the Son, and to the spirit of both. The fatherhood of the Father meets and blends with the sonhood of the Son. It draws us up into the glory of their joy. They invite us to share in the thoughts of love that pass between them, in their thoughts of delight and rest in each, in their thoughts of joy in all the little ones.

The life of Jesus is the light of men, revealing to them the Father.

— THE SUPREME ACTION OF LIFE —

But light is not enough. Light exists for the sake of life. We too must have life in ourselves. We too, like the Life himself, must live. We can live in no way but that in which Jesus lived, in which life was made in him.

That way is to give up our life. This is the one supreme action of life possible to us for the making of life in ourselves. Christ did it of himself, and so became light to us that we might be able to do it in ourselves, after him, and through his originating act.

I repeat: We must do it ourselves. The help that he has given and gives, the light and the spirit-working of the Lord, the spirit, in our hearts, is all in order that we may, as we must, do it ourselves. Till then we are not alive. Life is not made in us.

The whole strife and labour and agony of the Son with every man is to get him to die as he died. All preaching that aims not at this is a building with wood and hay and stubble.

If I say not with my whole heart, "My Father, do with me as you will, only help me against myself and for you," then his life is not yet fully alive in me.

If I cannot say, "I am your child, the inheritor of your spirit, your being, a part of yourself, glorious in you, but grown poor in me—let me be your dog, your horse, your anything you will . . . let me be yours in any shape the love that is my Father may please to have me, let me be yours in any way, and my own in no way but yours"—if we cannot as fully as this give ourselves to the Father, then we have not yet laid hold upon that for which Christ has laid hold upon us.

The faith that a man may—nay, must—put in God reaches above earth and sky. It stretches beyond the farthest outlying star of the creatable universe. The question is not at present, however, of removing mountains, a thing that will one day be simple to us, but of waking and rising from the dead *now*.

When a man truly and perfectly says with Jesus, and as Jesus said it, "Thy will be done," he closes the everlasting life-circle. The life of the Father and the Son flows through him. He is a part of the divine organism. Then is the prayer of the Lord in him fulfilled: "I in them and thou in me that they may be made perfect in one."

The Christ in us is the spirit of the perfect child toward the perfect father. The Christ in us is our own true nature made to blossom within us by the Lord, whose life is the light of men, that it may become the life of men. Our true nature is childhood to the Father.

— LET US ARISE AND LIVE —

Friends, those of you who know or suspect that these things are true, let us arise and live. Let us arise even in the darkest moments of spiritual lethargy, when hope itself sees nothing to hope for. Let us not trouble ourselves about the cause of our earthliness, except we know it to be some unrighteousness in us, but let us go at once to the Life.

Never, never let us accept as consolation the poor suggestion that the cause of our deadness is physical. It is no comfort to know that this body of ours, because of the death in it, is too much for the spirit—for the spirit ought not merely to triumph over the body but to inspire it with subjection and obedience. Let us comfort ourselves rather in the thought of the Father and the Son. So long as there dwells harmony, so long as the Son loves the Father with all the love the Father can welcome, all is well with their little ones.

God is all right. Therefore, why should we mind standing in the dark for a minute outside his window? Of course we miss the *inness*. But there is a bliss of its own in waiting. What if the rain be falling, and the wind blowing? What if we stand alone, or, more painful still, have some dear one beside us, sharing our *outness*? What even if the window be not shining because of the curtains of impenetrable good drawn across it? Let us think to ourselves, or say to our friend, "God is. Jesus is not dead. Nothing can be going wrong, however it may look to our hearts that are unfinished in childness."

Let us say to the Lord, "Jesus, are you loving the Father in there? Then we out here will do his will, patiently waiting till he open the door. We shall not mind the wind or the rain much. For perhaps you are saying to the Father, *Your little ones need some wind and rain. Their buds are hard. The flowers do not come out. I cannot get them to be made blessed without a little more winter weather.* Then perhaps the Father will say, *Comfort them, my son Jesus, with the memory of your patience when you were missing me. Comfort them that you were*

*sure of me when everything about you seemed so unlike
me, so unlike the place you had left."*

In a word, let us be at peace, because peace is at the
heart of things—peace and utter satisfaction between
the Father and the Son—in which peace they call us to
share, in which peace they promise that at length, when
they have their good way with us, we *shall* share.

Before us, then, lies a bliss unspeakable. It is a bliss
beyond the thought or invention of man. It is offered to
every child who will fall in with the perfect imagination
of the Father. His imagination is one with his creative
will. Whatever God imagines, that thing exists.

When the created falls in with the will of him who
"loved him into being," then all is well. Thenceforward
the mighty creation goes on in him upon higher and yet
higher levels, in more and yet more divine airs.

*Thy will, O God, be done! Nothing else is other than
loss, decay, and corruption. There is no life but that born
of the life that the Word made in himself by doing thy
will, which life is the light of men. Through that light is
born the life of men—the same life in them that came first
into being in Jesus. As he laid down his life, so must we
lay down our lives, that as he lives we may live also. That
which was made in him was life, and the life is the light
of men.*

Insights Into

The Creation
in Christ

MICHAEL PHILLIPS

— WHY COMMENTARIES? —

George MacDonald is a writer who can be read on
many levels. This explains why he has had loyal readers
spanning as broad a spectrum as does his protégé C. S.
Lewis. It also explains why he has been such a literary,
theological, and personal spiritual force in the lives of so
many thousands since he began his professional literary
career more than one hundred fifty years ago.

Within that broad range of readership there will be
those who disparage the idea of redacting MacDonald's
nonfiction writings, feeling that the originals should be
good enough for everyone, no matter how difficult they
may be to wade through. Others, though happy to read

these redacted editions, will question the need for commentary to supplement them.

It is not for such that I add these thoughts of my own to this and succeeding chapters. I present these insights, for what they happen to be worth, for those readers who may perhaps find them helpful.

Many readers of MacDonald's novels find themselves hungering for a succinct representation of his thought, his outlook, his view of God. Such is not to be found in any single piece of writing from his pen. The books of this series of writings, taken as a whole, likely come as close as it is possible to get.

George MacDonald's boldest ideas come to us in five nonfiction volumes published during his lifetime. These were called *Unspoken Sermons* (1867), *The Miracles of Our Lord* (1870), *Unspoken Sermons, Second Series* (1885), *Unspoken Sermons, Third Series* (1889), and *The Hope of the Gospel* (1892). Most of the chapters in the books of this series comprise a single chapter from one of those five volumes.

MacDonald also wrote a volume the contents of which varies slightly with differing editions, variously titled *Orts, Chiefly Papers on the Imagination, and On Shakspere* (1882), *The Imagination and Other Essays* (1883—American edition), and *A Dish of Orts* (1893—"enlarged edition"). Some chapters of interest from that work are included in this series as well.

— THE BOLD FOUNDATION OF —
A PRACTICAL THEOLOGY

This series begins with the excerpt from *Unspoken Sermons, Third Series* entitled "The Creation in Christ."

That selection represents a foundation stone, perhaps *the* foundation stone, of MacDonald's perspective on God and his work, and, significantly, his perspective on man's pivotal role in that eternal work in which God is engaged. This single chapter—upon which MacDonald embarks by questioning whether the translation of John 1:3–4 as given in the King James, or, in his day, the "Authorized Version," is in fact a proper rendition of John's intended meaning—contains unfathomable depths to illuminate the relationship between God and his highest creation. Furthermore, it explores the foundations of God's multi-faced nature, and the distinctive purposes and works of those personal aspects of the Creator that have been revealed to us.

I consider "The Creation in Christ" one of MacDonald's most original and theologically courageous works, placing him in the first rank of history's Christian thinkers. The thought-progressions he communicates here stand at the core of his life and faith. In it he examines the very heart of the Godhead and the origins of creation itself, delving into the mysteries of the unique roles occupied by the Father and the Son.

It may be rigorous going for some. It has been for me. This is not milk but strong spiritual meat. I encourage you to stick with it. Many of these passages required three or four readings in the original before the light began to dawn in my understanding of what MacDonald was attempting to communicate. He is here probing the deepest depths of our faith. If it takes some mental horsepower to keep with him, our efforts are well worth it.

It may be daring to say, and I may open myself to criticism for doing so, but I truly feel that MacDonald's bold and magnificent insights place the revelations in this and in many of those selections that will follow alongside the book of Romans in potential significance for the Christian who would fathom what the Father and the Son are to us, and how their joint creative work ought to affect every moment of our lives.

Perhaps this assessment overstates the case. God knows. But such a claim reflects something of the profound impact this sermon has exercised on my own perspective of Christ's ongoing work.

— THE HEART OF THE GODHEAD —

After sharing his thoughts on John 1:3–4, MacDonald establishes the foundation for the discussion in which he intends to engage, the distinction between those things created *through* Christ and that which was created *in* Christ. It is the latter—that created *in* him, which God purposes also to be made alive in each one of us—which MacDonald will attempt to illuminate to our understanding.

To do so, and in order to discuss "creation" from a proper standpoint, he first distinguishes between the separate roles occupied in creation by the Father and the Son. Recognizing the controversial nature of an attempt to unravel any portion of the mystery of the Trinity (and emphasizing a recurrent MacDonald theme—a hatred of controversy and dispute over doctrinal matters), Mac-Donald nevertheless plunges into its depths, differentiating between Father and Son and the unique contribution each makes to their relationship, then explaining how what has been created *through* the Son differs from the ultimate creation that comes to life *in* the Son.

Thus MacDonald writes:

> I believe, then, that Jesus Christ is the eternal Son
> of the eternal Father. I believe that from the first
> beginnings of all things Jesus is the Son, because
> God is the Father. . . . I believe therefore that the
> Father is the greater, and that if the Father had not
> been, the Son could not have been. . . .
>
> I worship the Son as the human God, the
> divine, the only perfect Man. He derives his being
> and power from the Father, and is equal with him
> as a son is both the equal and at the same time the
> subject of his father. *Yet he makes himself the equal*
> *of his father only in what is most precious in the*
> *Godhead, namely, Love.* This . . . is a higher thing
> than the making of the worlds and the things in
> them, which making he did by the power of the
> Father, not by a self-existent power in himself. For
> this reason, the apostle . . . says, "All things were
> made" not *by*, but "*through* him." . . .
>
> The Father, in bringing out of the unseen the
> things that are seen, made essential use of the Son.
> All that exists, therefore, was created *through* him.
> What may be the difference between the part in
> creation of the Father and the part of the Son, who
> can understand? Perhaps we may one day come to
> see into it a little.

He goes on to explain that in addition to those things
made *through* the Son, there was also something made
in him, a different kind of *life* than the material creation
of the universe, a kind of life, if we are able to grasp it,
that we may partake of.

— THE LIFE MADE *IN* JESUS —

What is this special kind of *life?* MacDonald asks. It is not merely the life of being born again, as many might suppose. This different kind of life is far more than salvation itself, which is but one small aspect of it. "Many forms of life have come to being *through* the Son," he says. But what is the life that has been made *in* him?

It is simply this: The capacity and power to choose *another* will than our own—a higher will, God's will—and make it our own in place of our own.

It is this that Jesus, as the Son, did.

In so doing, he created in himself, by the free choice of perfect love, a new form of life—the life of laying down his own will and taking upon himself the will of the Father. This is the life in the Son that corresponds to the creating power of the Father. The two forms of love in the Godhead—*creating* love and *self-denying* love—mirror one another yet reveal the same source of love. The Father's love is outgoing, while the Son's love responds by deathing his own motives into the love of the Father.

This is the ultimate sonship, the ultimate childship.

> The life of Christ is this: negatively, that he does nothing, cares nothing for his own sake, and positively, that he cares with his whole soul for the will and pleasure of his father. Because his father is his father, therefore he will be his *child.*

— FROM HIM TO US —

From this foundation, MacDonald moves toward the pinnacle of his intended purpose. That same life made "in" Christ and demonstrated and lived out every moment, by every breath Jesus took, is to be *our* life too. We make it our life in the same way Jesus made it his. And when we make it our life, it will indeed, as John says, be the light of men.

> The truth in Jesus is his relation to his father. The righteousness of Jesus is his fulfillment of that relation. . . . Giving himself with perfect will to God, choosing to die to himself and live to God, he therein creates in himself a new and higher life. Standing upon himself, he has gained the power to awaken life, the divine shadow of his own, in the hearts of us his brothers and sisters. We have come from the same birth-home as himself, namely, the heart of his God and our God, his father and our father. But without our elder brother to do it first, we would never have chosen that self-abjuration which is life, and never have become alive like him.
>
> To will, not from self, but with the Eternal, is to live.

MacDonald reaches his triumphant conclusion in one of the most powerful and significant passages in all his work:

> This choice of his own being, in the full knowledge of what he did—this active willing to be the Son of the Father, perfect in *obedience*—is that in Jesus which responds and corresponds to the self-existence of God. Jesus rose at once to the height of his being and set himself down on the throne of his nature in the act of *subjecting* himself to the will of

the Father as his only good, the only *reason* of his existence. When he died on the cross, he did . . . that which he had done at home in glory and gladness. From the infinite beginning—for here I can speak only by contradictions—he completed and held fast the eternal circle of his existence in saying, *"Thy will, not mine, be done!"*

He made himself what he is by deathing himself into the will of the eternal Father, through which will he was the eternal Son—thus plunging into the fountain of his own life, the everlasting Fatherhood, and taking the Godhead of the Son.

— THE POWER OF CHOOSING —

How do we enter into such creative life in Christ ourselves?

MacDonald says it clearly. We must *choose* it. Jesus originates the possibility of *our* choosing in *his* choosing. We take it for ourselves by choosing it also, just as he chose it and continues to choose it, every moment. We do so in our will. This is a vastly different thing than what is commonly called "salvation" according to ideas of belief or "plans of salvation" as MacDonald elsewhere calls them. He is here speaking, rather, of laying down self-will in all things and in all ways, a result which may or may not accompany even the most right and correct "ideas" of belief. It is also a very different thing than that orientation which assumes that all the work of spiritual growth within the Christian is *God's* alone to carry out through the operation of grace. Instead, here, as everywhere, MacDonald places the responsibility for our inward development of childness on *our* shoulders.

We must *will* ourselves to be children.

> Because we are come out of the divine nature, which chooses to be divine, we also must *choose* to be divine. We must choose to be of God, to be one with God. We must choose to love and live as he loves and lives. . . .
>
> Man cannot originate this life. It must be shown him, and he must choose it. God is the father of Jesus and of us—of every possibility of our being. But while God is the father of his children, Jesus is the father of their childship. . . .
>
> We are not and cannot become true sons without our will willing his will. Our doing follows his making. It was the will of Jesus to be what God willed and meant him to be that made him the true son of God. . . . So with us: We must *be* the sons and daughters we are. . . . We must *be* sons and daughters in our will.
>
> And we can be sons and daughters . . . only by choosing God for the father he is and by doing his will—yielding ourselves as true sons to the absolute Father. Therein lies the only and essential human bliss.

And when we do, this life becomes our light.

The Son's willfully chosen death to self-motive into the will of the Father is the unity in which Jesus prayed we would walk with him. It is this unity of love and devotion which MacDonald calls "the bond of the universe," magnificently arriving at the mountain-peak of his thought progression:

The bond of the universe, the chain that holds it together, the one active unity, the harmony of things . . . is the devotion of the Son to the Father. . . . It is the life of the universe.

It is not the fact that God created all things that makes the universe a whole. It is rather that he through whom he created them loves him perfectly and is eternally content in his father and satisfied to be because his father is with him. . . . The eternal fact is that God and Christ are one. They are father and son. The Father loves the Son as only the Father can love. The Son loves the Father as only the Son can love. . . .

We can live in no way but that in which Jesus lived, in which life was made in him.

That way is to give up our life. This is the one supreme action of life possible to us for the making of life in ourselves. Christ did it of himself, and so became light to us that we might be able to do it in ourselves, after him, and through his originating act.

I repeat: We must do it ourselves. . . .

When a man truly and perfectly says with Jesus, and as Jesus said it, "Thy will be done," he closes the everlasting life-circle. The life of the Father and the Son flows through him. He is a part of the divine organism. Then is the prayer of the Lord in him fulfilled: "I in them and thou in me that they may be made perfect in one."

The Christ in us is the spirit of the perfect child toward the perfect father. . . . Our true nature is childhood to the Father.

As we continue to explore George MacDonald's writings, we will find ourselves returning to this same theme over and over again. We will discover this perspective between the lines of every subject under consideration. It is foundational in MacDonald's view of the *Father's* infinite and outflowing love, the *Son's* infinite and self-abnegating devotion, and *man's* infinite opportunity and personal responsibility to live in self-willed and chosen childship, sharing with Jesus the creation in Christ which his own self-denial and loving obedience makes possible.

I came that they may have life, and may have it abundantly.

—JOHN 10:10

Life

GEORGE MACDONALD

The life the Lord came to give us is a life exceeding that of the highest undivine man by far more than the life of that man exceeds the life of the least human animal. More and more of that life exists for each who will receive it, and that to eternity.

In a word, Jesus came to supply all our lack—from the root outward. And what we need is more life.

— LIFE, NOT DEATH —

What does the infant need but more life? What does the bosom of his mother give him but life in abundance?

What does the old man need, whose limbs are weak and whose pulse is low, but more of the life which seems ebbing from him? Weary with feebleness, he calls upon death, but in reality it is *life* he wants. It is but the

encroaching death in him that desires death. He longs
for rest, but death cannot rest. Death would be as much
an end to rest as to weariness. Even weakness cannot
rest. It takes strength as well as weariness to rest.

How different is the weariness of the strong man
after prolonged labour from the weariness of the sick
man who in the morning cries out, "Would God it were
evening!" and in the evening, "Would God it were
morning!"

Low-sunk life imagines itself weary of life. But it is
death, not life, it is weary of. Never a cry went out after
the opposite of life from any soul that knew what life is.
Why does the poor, worn suicide seek death? Is it not in
reality to escape from death—from the death of home-
lessness and hunger and cold, the death of failure and
disappointment and distraction, the death of the
exhaustion of passion, the death of crime and fear of discovery, the death of madness—of a household he cannot
rule? He seeks the darkness because it seems a refuge
from the death which possesses him. He is a creature
possessed by death. What he calls his life is but a dream
full of horrible phantasms.

More life! is the unconscious prayer of all creation,
groaning and travailing for the redemption of its lord,
the son who is not yet a son. Can we not read the same
silent cry in the faces of some of the animals, in the look
in some of the flowers, and in many an aspect of what
we call Nature?

— THE CREATION OF SEPARATION —
AND INDIVIDUALITY

All things are possible with God, but all things are
not easy. It is easy for him *to be*, for there he has to do

with his own perfect will. It is not easy for him to create—that is, after the grand fashion which alone will satisfy his glorious heart and will, the fashion in which he
is now creating us.

In the very nature of being—that is, God—it must
be hard (and divine history shows how hard) to create
that which shall be not himself, yet like himself. The
problem is to separate from himself that which must yet
be ever and always and utterly dependent on him, and
to separate it sufficiently that it shall have the existence
of a free individual. Only so shall it be able to turn and
regard him—choose him, and say, "I will arise and go to
my Father." Only so shall it develop in itself the highest
Divine of which it is capable—the will able to side with
the good against the evil, the will to be one with the life
whence it has come and in which it still is.

This highest Divine expresses itself as the will to
close the round of its procession in its return, so working
the perfection of reunion—to shape in its own life the
ring of eternity. In doing so it chooses to live immediately, consciously, and active-willingly from its source,
from its own very life—to restore to the beginning the
end that comes of that beginning—to be the thing the
Maker thought of when he willed, before he began to
work its being.

I imagine the difficulty of doing this thing, of effect-
ing this creation, this separation from himself such that
will in the creature be possible—I imagine, I say, the difficulty of such creation so great that for it God must
begin inconceivably far back in the infinitesimal regions
of beginnings. I do not say merely before the existence
of anything in the least resembling man, but eternal
miles beyond the last farthest-pushed discovery in

protoplasm. It must have been in *infinite* beginnings
when God set in motion that division from himself
which in its grand result should be individuality, consciousness, choice, and conscious choice—choice at last
pure because it is the choice of the right, the true, the
divinely harmonious.

Hence the final end of the separation is not individuality. That is but a means to it. The final end is oneness—an impossibility without the prior separation. For
there can be no unity, no delight of love, no harmony, no
good in being, where there is but one. Two at least are
needed for oneness. And the greater the number of individuals, the greater, the lovelier, the richer, the diviner
is the possible unity.

God is life, and the will-source of life. In the outflowing of that life, I know him. And when I am told
that he is love, I see that if he were not love he could
not create. I know nothing deeper in him than love. I
believe there is nothing in him deeper than love—nay,
that there *can* be anything deeper than love.

The being of God is love, therefore he creates. I
imagine that from all eternity he has been creating. As
he saw it was not good for man to be alone, so has he
never been alone himself. From all eternity the Father
has had the Son. And the never-begun existence of that
Son I imagine an easy outgoing of the Father's nature.
To make other beings, however, beings like us, I imagine
the labour of God to be an eternal labour. Speaking after
our poor human fashions of thought—the only fashions
possible to us—I imagine that God has never been content to be alone even with the Son of his love, the prime
and perfect idea of humanity. I imagine that from the
first he has willed and laboured to give existence to

other creatures who should be blessed with his blessedness—creatures whom he is now and always has been developing into likeness with that Son. It is a likeness seemingly for eons distant and small, but a likeness forever growing. Perhaps never one of them yet, though unspeakably blessed, has had even an approximate idea of the blessedness in store for him.

— GOD'S PAIN TO GIVE US LIFE —

Let no one think that to say God undertook a hard labour in willing that many sons and daughters should be sharers of the divine nature is to lessen his glory! The greater the difficulty, the greater is the glory of him who does the thing he has undertaken—without shadow of compromise, with no half-success, but with a triumph of absolute satisfaction to innumerable radiant souls! God knew what it would cost—not energy of will alone, or merely that utterance and separation from himself which is but the first of creation, though that may well itself be pain. He knew also that it would cost a sore suffering such as we cannot imagine, suffering that could only be God's, in the bringing out—call it birth or development—of the God-life in the individual soul. It is a suffering ever renewed in God's heart, a labour continually thwarted by that soul itself, compelling God to take, still at the cost of his own suffering, the not absolutely best, only the best possible means left him by the resistance of his creature.

Man finds it hard to get what he wants because he does not want the best. God finds it hard to give because he would give the best, and man will not take it. What Jesus did was what the Father is always doing. The suffering he endured was that of the Father from the foundation of the world, reaching its climax in the person of his son.

— THE SACRIFICE IS HIMSELF —

God provides the sacrifice. The sacrifice is himself.

He is always, and has ever been, sacrificing himself to and for his creatures. It lies in the very essence of his creation of them. The worst heresy, next to that of dividing religion and righteousness, is to divide the Father from the Son—in thought or feeling or action or intent, to represent the Son as doing that which the Father does not himself do.

Jesus did nothing but what the Father did and does. If Jesus suffered for men, it was because his father suffers for men. Jesus came close to men, through his body and their senses, that he might bring their spirits close to his father and their father and, by losing what could be lost of his own, so give them life.

He is God our Saviour. It is because God is our Saviour that Jesus is our Saviour. The God and Father of Jesus Christ could never possibly be satisfied with less than giving himself to his own! The unbeliever may easily imagine a better God than the prevailing theology of his culture offers him. But the lovingest heart that ever beat cannot even fathom the length and breadth and depth and height of that love of God which shows itself in his Son—one, and of one mind, with himself. The whole history is a divine agony to give divine life to creatures. The outcome of that agony, the victory of that creative and continually creative energy, will be radiant life, whereof joy unspeakable is the flower. Every child will look into the eyes of the Father, and the eyes of the Father will receive the child with an infinite embrace.

This life exists for all who will receive it. The Father has given to the Son to have life in himself. That life is our light. We know life only as light. It is the life in us that makes us see. All the growth of the Christian is the more and more life he is receiving. At first his religion may hardly be distinguishable from the mere prudent desire to save his soul. But eventually he loses that very soul in the glory of love, and so saves it. Self becomes but the cloud on which the white light of God divides into harmonies unspeakable.

"In the midst of life we are in death," said one. It is more true that in the midst of death we are in life. Life is the only reality. What men call death is but a shadow—a word for that which cannot be, a negation which owes the very idea of itself to that which it would deny. But for life there could be no death. If God did not exist, there would not even be nothing. Not even nothingness preceded life. Nothingness owes its very idea to existence.

— MORE LIFE —

One form of the question between matter and spirit is, which existed first and caused the other—things or thoughts? Did things without thought cause thought? Or did thought without things cause things?

To those who cannot doubt that thought was first, causally preceding the earliest manifestation of the material universe, it is plain that death can be the cure for nothing. The cure for everything must be life. The ills which come with existence come from its imperfection, not of existence itself. What we need is more of it, not less. We who exist have nothing to do with death. Our relations are alone with life. The thing that can mourn can mourn only from lack. It cannot mourn because of being but because of not enough of being.

We are vessels of life, but we are not yet full of the wine of life. Where the wine does not reach, there the clay cracks and aches and is distressed. Who would therefore pour out the wine that is there instead of filling the cup to the brim with more wine!

All the being must partake of essential being. Life must be assisted, upheld, comforted, every part, with life. Life is the law, the food, the necessity of life. Life is everything.

Many mistake the joy of life for life itself. Longing after the joy, they languish with a thirst that is poor and inextinguishable. But even that thirst points to the one spring. Such as these love self, not life, and self is but the shadow of life. When it is taken for life itself, and set as the man's centre, it becomes a live death in the man—a devil he worships as his god.

The soul compact of harmonies has more life, a larger being, than the soul consumed of cares. The sage is a larger life than the clown. The poet is more alive than the man whose life flows out that money may come in. The man who loves his fellow is infinitely more alive than he whose endeavour is to exalt himself above him. The man who strives to be better is aliver than he who longs for the praise of the many.

But the man to whom God is all in all, who feels his life-roots hid with Christ in God, who knows himself the inheritor of all wealth, worlds, ages, and power— that man has begun to be alive indeed.

— COURAGE TO FIGHT FOR LIFE —

Let us in all the troubles of life remember that our one lack is life, that what we need is more life—more of the life-making presence in us making us more, and more largely, alive.

When most oppressed, when most weary of life, as our unbelief would phrase it, let us remind ourselves that it is in truth the inroad and presence of death we are weary of. When most inclined to sleep, let us rouse ourselves to live. Of all things let us avoid the false refuge of a weary collapse, a hopeless yielding to things as they are. It is the life in us that is discontented. We need more of what is discontented, not more of the cause of its discontent.

Discontent, I repeat, is the life in us that has not enough of itself. He has the victory who, in the midst of pain and weakness, cries out, not for death or for the repose of forgetfulness, but for strength to fight, for more power, more consciousness of being, more God in him. He has the victory who, when sorely wounded, says with Sir Andrew Barton in the old ballad:

Fight on my men, says Sir Andrew Barton,
I am hurt, but I am not slain;
I'll lay me down and bleed awhile,
And then I'll rise and fight again.

We summon such courage with no silly notion of playing the hero—what have creatures like us who are not yet barely honest to do with heroism!—but because so to fight is the truth, and the only way to live.

If in the extreme of our exhaustion there should

come to us, as to Elijah when he slept in the desert, an angel to rouse us and show us the waiting bread and water, how would we carry ourselves? Would we remain faint and unwilling to rise and eat? Would we answer, *Lo, I am weary unto death! The battle is gone from me! It is lost, or not worth gaining! The world is too much for me! Its forces will not heed me! They have worn me out! I have wrought no salvation even for my own, and never should work any, were I to live for ever! It is enough. Let me now return whence I came. Let me be gathered to my fathers and be at rest.*

I should be loath to think that, if the enemy, in recognizable shape, came roaring upon us, we would not, like the red-cross knight, stagger, heavy sword in nerveless arm, to meet him. In the feebleness of foiled effort, it requires yet more faith to rise and partake of the food that shall bring back more effort, more travail, more weariness.

The true man trusts in a strength which is not his and which he does not feel—which he does not even always desire. He believes in a power that seems far from him which is yet at the root of his fatigue itself and his need of rest—rest as far from death as is labour.

To trust in the strength of God in our weakness is victory. To say, *I am weak: so let me be. God is strong,* is victory. To seek from him who is our life, as the natural, simple cure of all that is amiss with us, the power to *do,* and *be,* and *live,* even when we are weary—this is the victory that overcomes the world.

To believe in God our strength in the face of all seeming denial . . . to believe in him out of the heart of weakness and unbelief in spite of numbness and weariness and lethargy . . . to believe in the wide-awake *real,* through all the stupefying, enervating, distorting dream . . . to will to wake when the very being seems athirst for a godless repose—these are the broken steps up to the high fields where repose is but a form of strength, strength but a form of joy, joy but a form of love.

"I am weak," says the true soul, "but not so weak that I would not be strong, not so sleepy that I would not see the sun rise, not so lame but that I would walk! Thanks be to him who perfects strength in weakness, and gives to his beloved while they sleep!"

If we will but let our God and Father work his will with us, there can be no limit to his enlargement of our existence, to the flood of life with which he will overflow our consciousness. We have no conception of what life might be, of how vast the consciousness of which we could be made capable.

Many can recall some moment in which life seemed richer and fuller than ever before. To some such moments arrive mostly in dreams. But shall a soul, awake or asleep, embrace a greater bliss than its Life, the living God, can seal, perpetuate, and enlarge? Can the human twilight of a dream be capable of generating or holding a fuller life than the morning of divine reality? Surely God could at any moment give to a soul, by a word breathing afresh into the secret caves of that soul's being, a sense of life before which the most exultant ecstasy of earthly triumph would pale to ashes!

If ever sunlit, sail-crowded sea, under blue heaven flecked with wind-chased white, filled your heart as with a new gift of life, think what sense of existence must be yours if he whose thought has but fringed its garment with the outburst of such a show make his home with you. And while imagining the gladness of God inside your being, think of the wonder that he is carrying you as a father in his bosom!

— THE DIFFERENCE BETWEEN LOW — CONSCIOUSNESS AND TRUE LIFE

I have been speaking as if *life* and *awareness of life* were one. But the consciousness of life is not itself life, it is only the outcome of life. The *real* "life" is that which exists of and by itself—which *is*, that is, which exists in the active rather than the passive sense. Such life can only be God. But there ought to be in us a life correspondent to the life that is God's. There also must be in us a form of life able to will itself—a life resembling the self-existent life of God, and partaking sufficiently of it that it is capable of taking a share in its own being.

There is an original act possible to man which must initiate the reality of his existence. He must live by *willing* himself to live.

A tree "lives." Perhaps it has some vague consciousness, known *by* but not *to* itself, known only to the God who made it. I trust that life in its lowest forms is on the way to thought and blessedness, is in the process of that separation, so to speak, from God, in which consists the creation of living souls.

But the life of these lower forms is not *life* in the high sense—in the sense in which the word is used in the Bible. True life *knows* and *rules* itself. The eternal life is life come awake. Whatever it may one day become, and however I may refuse to believe their fate and being fixed as we see them, the life of the most exalted of the animals is not such as this at present. No man or woman would be inclined to call the existence of the dog, looking unknowingly up out of his wistful eyes, an existence to be satisfied with, or would call his life an end sufficient in itself.

But I would just as little look on the human pleasure, the human refinement, the common human endeavour around me, and regard them as worthy of the word *life*. What is true in them dwells amidst an unchallenged corruption—a corruption that demands repentance and labour and prayer for its destruction. The condition of most men and women seems to me a life in death, an abode in unwhited sepulchers, a possession of withering forms by spirits that slumber and babble in their dreams.

Of course, they do not feel it so. But that means nothing. The sow wallowing in the mire may rightly assert it her way of being clean, but theirs is not the life of the God-born. The day must come when they will hide their faces with such shame as the good man yet feels at the memory of the time when he lived like them.

— GOD'S LIFE —

There is nothing for man worthy to be called *life* but life eternal—God's life, that is, after his degree shared by the man made to be eternal also. For he is in the image of God, intended to partake of the life of the most high, to be alive as he is alive. Of this life the outcome and the light is righteousness, love, grace, truth. But the *life* itself is a thing that is not so easily defined, even as God will not be defined. It is a power, the formless cause of form. It has no limits whereby to be defined. It shows itself to the soul that is hungering and thirsting after righteousness. But that soul cannot show it to another, except in the shining of its own light.

When he hears of what is called "eternal life," the ignorant soul thinks of it only in the sense of duration, as an endless elongation of consciousness. What God means by it, however, is to live as a being like his own, a being beyond the attack of decay or death, a being so essential that it has no relation whatever to nothingness. By *life*, God means that which is, and can never go to that which is not, for with that it never had to do, but came out of the heart of Life, the heart of God, the fountain of being. By *life*, God means an existence that partakes of the divine nature, and that has nothing in common, any more than the Eternal himself, with what can pass or cease. God owes his being to no one, and his child has no lord but his father.

This life, this eternal life, consists for man in absolute oneness with God and all divine modes of being, oneness with every phase of right and harmony. It consists in a love as deep as it is universal, as conscious as it is unspeakable. It consists of a love that can no more be reasoned about than life itself—a love whose presence is its all-sufficing proof and justification, whose absence is an annihilating defect. He who does not have it cannot believe in it. How can death believe in life, though all the birds of God are singing jubilant over the empty tomb! The delight of such a being, the splendour of a consciousness rushing from the wide-open doors of the fountain of existence, the ecstasy of the spiritual sense into which the surge of life essential, immortal, increate, flows in silent fullness from the heart of hearts—what may it, what must it not be, in the great day of God and the individual soul!

— OUR PRACTICAL RESPONSE —

What then is our practical relation to God and his life original?

What is our part toward the attaining to the resurrection from the dead? If we did not make ourselves, and *could not* have made ourselves, now that we are made, are we capable of accomplishing anything at the unknown roots of our being? What relation of conscious unity can exist between the self-existent God and beings such as ourselves who live at the will of another? Indeed, even if we do not acknowledge the relation, we are beings who cannot even refuse to be. We cannot even cease to be. We must, at the will of that other who made us, go on living, weary of what is not life. We are able to assert our relation to life only by refusing to be content with what is not life.

We live by the will of the self-existent God. The links of unity with him already exist within us. All they need is to be brought together. In order to find the link in our being with which to close the circle of immortal oneness with the Father, we must of course search the deepest of man's nature. There only can it be found.

And there we do find it. For the *will* is the deepest, the strongest, the divinest thing in man. So, I presume, is it in God, for such we find it in Jesus Christ. Here, and here only, in the relation of the two wills, God's and his own, can a man come into vital contact with the All-in-all. And it is no one-sided unity of complete dependence but is the eternal idea of willed harmony of dual oneness. When a man can and does entirely say, *Not my will, but thine be done*—when he so wills the will of God as to do it—then is he one with God, one as a true son with a true father.

God's life within him is the causing and bearing of his life. It is therefore absolutely and only of its kind, one with it more and deeper than words or figures can say. It is the life which is itself, only more of itself, and, more than that, which *causes* itself. When a man wills that his being be conformed to that being of his origin, which is the life in his life, when a man thus accepts his own causing life, *and sets himself to live the will of that causing life*, humbly eager after the privileges of his origin, he thus receives God's life into himself. He becomes, in the act, a partaker of the divine nature, a true son of the living God, and an heir of all he possesses. By the obedience of a son, he receives into himself the very life of the Father.

Obedience is the joining of the links of the eternal round. Obedience is but the other side of the creative will. Will is God's will, obedience is man's will. The two make one. The root-life, knowing well the thousand troubles it would bring upon him, has created and goes on creating other lives, that, though incapable of self-being, they may, by willed obedience, share in the bliss of his essential self-ordained being.

If we do the will of God, eternal life is ours. It is no mere continuity of existence, for that in itself is worthless as hell. Rather it is a being that is one with God's essential life, and so able to fill us with the abundant and endless outgoings of his life. Our souls shall thus become vessels ever growing. And ever as they grow shall they be filled with more and more life proceeding from the

Father and the Son, from God the ordaining and God the obedient.

We can never know the delight of the being or the abundance of the life he came to give us until we have it. But even now to the holy imagination it may sometimes seem too glorious—as if we must die of very life . . . of more being than we could bear—to think of awaking to this higher life and being filled with a wine which our souls were heretofore too weak to hold!

To be for one moment aware of such pure, simple love toward but one of my fellows, as I trust I shall one day have toward each, must of itself bring a sense of life such as the utmost effort of my imagination can but feebly now begin to shadow. What a mighty glory of consciousness! Yet that glory I now feel in the mere idea of it will not even always be present. For my love, indeed, and not my glory in it, will be my life. There would be, even in that one love, in the simple purity of a single affection such as we were created to generate and intended to cherish toward all, an expansion of life inexpressible, unutterable.

For we are made for love, not for self. Our neighbour is our refuge. *Self* is our demon-foe. Every man is the image of God to every man, and in proportion as we love him, we shall know the sacred fact. The precious thing to the human soul is, and one day shall be known to be, every other human soul.

And if it be so between man and man, how will it not be between the man and his Maker, between the child and his eternal Father, between the created and the creating Life? Must not the glory of existence be endlessly redoubled in the infinite love of the creature—for all love is infinite—to the infinite God, the great one Life, than whom is no other but only shadows, lovely shadows of him!

Reader to whom my words seem those of inflation and foolish excitement, it can be nothing to you to be told that to my own ears I speak only the words of sober truth. May I pose this to you: Might the reason they seem foolish and exaggerated to your mind be not merely that you are not whole but that your being does not thirst after harmony and that you are not of the truth? If this be so, then you have not yet begun to live.

How should the reveller, coming worn and wasted out from the haunts where the violent seize joy by force to find her perish in their arms—how should such reveller, I say, break forth and sing with the sons of the morning when the ocean of light bursts from the fountain of the east? As little can you, with your mind full of petty cares, or still more petty ambitions, understand the groaning and travailing of the creation.

It may indeed be that you are honestly desirous of saving your own low soul. But as yet you can know but little of your need of him who is the very life within you. For we must do as the Master tells us, who knew all about the Father and the way to him—*we must deny ourselves, and take up our cross daily, and follow him.*

Insights Into
Life

MICHAEL PHILLIPS

— FEARLESS THEOLOGIAN —
WHO BROUGHT LIGHT

In "Life," from *Unspoken Sermons, Second Series,*
MacDonald continues and builds upon several of the
themes considered in "The Creation in Christ."

George MacDonald was a bold-thinking Christian
and a fearless theologian. It is remarkable to me to what
an extent *fear* still dominates much Christian thought.
This one of the two lies that Satan introduced into Eden
so long ago still infects Christendom like a silent, invisible cancer preventing us from knowing God fully. Not
only are we afraid to inquire high things of God ourselves, we condemn those who *do* think boldly of him,
calling them unorthodox if not outright heretics. This
disease of so-called "doctrinal purity," though truth is

obviously vital when properly understood, has come to replace obedience to the commands of Jesus as the authoritative validation of what constitutes "being a Christian." Thus, because it has been elevated to an exalted position far beyond what God intended, this thing we call doctrinal purity is *not* properly understood at all, and—the inevitable result when *anything* is made an idol—has become riddled with errors. It is neither pure nor, at many points, representative of right doctrine about God's being and work.

Laypersons and preachers and writers and theologians, however, cling to the leaky doctrinal lifeboats of their faith, as they consider it, circularly rowing in stagnant backwaters of belief, ignoring the invitation to board the magnificent vessel of bold and fearless faith that propelled the apostle Paul out into the waters where God's profoundest truths about himself are revealed.

George MacDonald—of course!—says it far more eloquently than I, using a related analogy to speak of "the man that holds by the mooring-ring of the letter, fast in the quay of what he calls theology, and from his rotting deck abuses the presumption of those that go down to the sea in ships. For such a one lets the wind of the spirit blow where it will, but never allows it to blow him out among its wonders in the deep" (from "The Knowing of the Son").

Much so-called theology is but an endless rehashing of what has come before. Men consider themselves "theologians" because they explain with a few novel words and expressions what has already been explained a thousand times. Most never offer a single new, innovative, thoughtful, imaginative, inspired *idea* to the tried and true "orthodoxy" that has been passed down to them by generations of preachers, priests, and theologians as unthinking as themselves.

And then came George MacDonald, sent to illuminate for us truths of God's nature and his work among us!

The light was not George MacDonald himself. But the three-sided prism of his *intellect,* his *heart,* and his *obedient nature* helped us to see truth as it was meant to be seen. As a result of his own determination to see clearly, unclouded from layers of orthodoxy dust and doctrinal haze from dull-thinking men, all three were pure enough to reflect and break down *God's* light into its constituent parts and translate that light to us in understandable forms in stories about people who understood how to live practically in the truth of that light.

MacDonald was *not* content to rehash what had been said before. He was bold to explore beyond the boundaries of the tentative and fearful, even beyond the boundaries of the "orthodox" if need be, and to suggest startlingly innovative ideas about God. In the midst of a nineteenth-century theology which viewed God, in MacDonald's words, as "the great and terrible sovereign," who else would dare pose instead the image of a child climbing into the smiling Father's lap and pulling his beard!

MacDonald hated controversy but did not fear it. He spoke the truth, and he let the truth within the hearts of his hearers determine the result.

> How terribly have the theologians misrepresented God. Nearly all of them represent him as a great

King on a grand throne, thinking how grand he is, and making it the business of his being and the end of his universe to keep up his glory, wielding the bolts of a Jupiter against them that take his name in vain.

They would not admit such a statement, but follow out what they say, and it amounts to this.

Brothers, have you found our king? There he is, kissing little children and saying they are like God. . . . For it is his childlikeness that makes him our God and Father (from "The Child in the Midst").

While others were content to talk *about* the Trinity, MacDonald delved into its midst in an attempt to shed light on the creating distinction between the Father and the Son: "I believe . . . that the Father is greater, and that if the Father had not been, the Son could not have been."

And in this selection we have just read, while others are content to talk *about* free will, MacDonald dares explore what he calls the "infinitesimal region of beginnings" of creation, speculating on how God could create beings that were both *dependent on him* and yet *sufficiently separate from him* to possess and exercise a wholly and entirely free will.

In both cases, the prism of MacDonald's mind, heart, and obedience offers imaginatively fresh insight into God's work and our necessary response. The exercise of this free will, seen in the light of MacDonald's illuminative understanding, is the essence of the *life* God has given mankind.

— THE MIRACLE OF CREATIVE SEPARATION —

We take a great deal about our systems of belief for granted because its ideas have come to us wrapped in the cloaks of generations-old orthodox explanations. Most of us desire comfort and warmth from the blankets themselves more than we desire the unshrouded crystalline purity of the truths they enclose. Religion ought to give comfort, it is true, and the truer the religion the more the comfort. But if we seek comfort *instead of* truth, that comfort we thought we had gained will one day evaporate in the consuming fire of the truth we ignored but will be able to disregard no longer.

Explanations are not truth, they are only explanations. And if they are low-minded explanations that make God's nature lower than that of the Father of Jesus Christ, then they are not even explanations of truth but explanations of *untruth*, and woe unto him who takes such and calls it "doctrinal purity."

Such it is for many Christians, I believe, with the two truths herein discussed: *being created in God's image* and *free will*.

MacDonald removes the explanatory, doctrinal, theological cloaks and asks, what do these two startling ideas really *mean* . . . practically?

Think what an incredible thing it is for God to create beings who are *like* him yet are so *separate* from him as to be able to reject him, and yet further whose only purpose in life is to choose to live in oneness with him . . . beings *capable* of evil, whose highest purpose is to *deny* the very evil they were made capable of. There is nothing else in all our experience, in all the universe, to correspond in any way to this utterly unique creation of likeness, separation, and distinct choice.

Does it not seem a very roundabout method for God to use to achieve his ends? Why did he not simply create beings to be like him and not capable of evil?

This is, of course, the great mystery. Concerning it, MacDonald adds what I find a remarkable comment, one that illuminates the originality of his thought concerning this kind of life that God brought into being.

He says that such a creation must have been hard.

All things are possible with God, but all things are not easy. It is easy for him *to be*, for there he has to do with his own perfect will. It is not easy for him to create—that is, after the grand fashion which alone will satisfy his glorious heart and will, the fashion in which he is now creating us.

In the very nature of being—that is, God—it must be hard (and divine history shows how hard) to create that which shall be not himself, yet like himself. The problem is to separate from himself that which must yet be ever and always and utterly dependent on him, and to separate it sufficiently that it shall have the existence of a free individual. Only so shall it be able to turn and regard him— choose him, and say, "I will arise and go to my Father." Only so shall it develop in itself the highest *Divine* of which it is capable—the will able to side with the good against the evil, the will to be one with the life whence it has come and in which it still is. . . . In doing so it chooses to live . . . active-willingly from its source.

— THE ROLE OF IMAGINATION IN —
UNDERSTANDING GOD'S NATURE

We now encounter another of MacDonald's unique-
nesses—his use of imagination to probe theological mysteries. One of the reasons he fell out of favor in his first
and only church and was effectively ousted from the
pulpit was that some in his congregation felt his imaginative and poetic bent indicated liberal theological lean-
ings. For MacDonald, however, the imagination was one
of God's primary gifts and tools given to enable us to
understand him more deeply and accurately. And here
MacDonald "imagines" something of God's creative
process to do this "difficult" thing.

> I imagine the difficulty of doing this thing, of
> effecting this creation, this separation from himself
> such that will in the creature be possible—I imag-
> ine, I say, the difficulty of such creation so great
> that for it God must begin inconceivably far back
> in the infinitesimal regions of beginnings. I do not
> say merely before the existence of anything in the
> least resembling man, but eternal miles beyond the
> last farthest-pushed discovery in protoplasm. It
> must have been in *infinite* beginnings when God set
> in motion that division from himself which in its
> grand result should be individuality, consciousness,
> choice, and conscious choice—choice at last pure
> because it is the choice of the right, the true, the
> divinely harmonious.

Why has God done this? Why has he divided his own
creation from himself by the gulf of separate free will?

For the purpose of having beings *separate* from him that are capable of growing into and expressing their *individuality* forever apart from him? No, it is for the purpose of *oneness*, the unity made possible both by the separation and the individuality.

> Hence the final end of the separation is not individuality—that is but a means to it. The final end is oneness—an impossibility without the prior separation. For there can be no unity, no delight of love, no harmony, no good in being, where there is but one. Two at least are needed for oneness. And the greater the number of individuals, the greater, the lovelier, the richer, the diviner is the possible unity.

Again MacDonald applies his imagination to reflect on the ongoing process required to create this unique form of separate, individual life with *unity* as its ultimate aim.

> The being of God is love, therefore he creates. I imagine that from all eternity he has been creating. As he saw it was not good for man to be alone, so has he never been alone himself. From all eternity the Father has had the Son. And the never-begun existence of that Son I imagine an easy outgoing of the Father's nature. To make other beings, however, beings like us, I imagine the labour of God to be an eternal labour. Speaking after our poor human fashions of thought . . . I imagine that God has never been content to be alone even with the Son of his love. . . . I imagine that from the first he has willed and laboured to give existence to other

creatures who should be blessed with his blessedness—creatures whom he is now and always has
been developing into likeness with that Son. It is a
likeness seemingly for eons distant and small, but a
likeness forever growing.

— PAIN AND SACRIFICE —

But this extraordinary creation—because it is a "difficult" creation, and because unity in the midst of separation and self-tending individuality is so hard a thing to
achieve—is not accomplished without pain.

> Let no one think that to say God undertook a hard
> labour in willing that many. sons and daughters
> should be sharers of the divine nature is to lessen
> his glory! The greater the difficulty, the greater is
> the glory of him who does the thing he has under-
> taken. . . . God knew what it would cost—not
> energy of will alone, or merely that utterance and
> separation from himself which is but the first of
> creation. . . . He knew also that it would cost a sore
> suffering such as we cannot imagine, suffering that
> could only be God's, in the . . . birth . . . of the
> God-life in the individual soul. It is a suffering ever
> renewed in God's heart, a labour continually
> thwarted by that soul itself, compelling God to
> take, still at the cost of his own suffering, the not
> absolutely best, only the best possible means left
> him by the resistance of his creature.

It is painful to God because, in the *individuality*
they imagine their own, his creatures do not want the

unity with their Creator they were created for and which can alone give them the life they think themselves capable of attaining without it.

> Man finds it hard to get what he wants because he does not want the best. God finds it hard to give because he would give the best, and man will not take it. What Jesus did was what the Father is always doing. The suffering he endured was that of the Father from the foundation of the world, reaching its climax in the person of his son.

And thus God sacrifices himself that man might be shown—by another man, a God-man—how to bridge the gap between individuality and unity, by saying across that seeming divide, and thus building a bridge for his own feet to cross it, "Not my will, but yours be done."

> God provides the sacrifice. The sacrifice is himself.
>
> He is always, and has ever been, sacrificing himself to and for his creatures. It lies in the very essence of his creation of them. The worst heresy, next to that of dividing religion and righteousness, is to divide the Father from the Son—in thought or feeling or action or intent, to represent the Son as doing that which the Father does not himself do.
>
> Jesus did nothing but what the Father did and does. If Jesus suffered for men, it was because his father suffers for men.

— WE MUST CHOOSE LIFE —

This is the life for which we were created as *individuals*—with individual and *separately* free wills com-

pletely our own—that we may die to those wills,
subserving them to the higher Will and saying, "I will
arise and go to my Father" to be my life. It is this *life*,
even in our weariness, doubt, and discontent, that our
souls long for.

> If we will but let our God and Father work his will
> with us, there can be no limit to his enlargement of
> our existence, to the flood of life with which he
> will overflow our consciousness. We have no con-
> ception of what life might be, of how vast the con-
> sciousness of which we could be made capable.

This is the true *life* that is beyond mere "awareness,"
a life that must rise and choose to *live*.

> I have been speaking as if *life* and *awareness of life*
> were one. But the consciousness of life is not itself
> life. . . . The *real* "life" is that which exists of and
> by itself. . . . Such life can only be God. But there
> ought to be in us a life correspondent to the life
> that is God's. There also must be in us a form of
> life able to will itself—a life resembling the self-
> existent life of God, and partaking sufficiently of it
> that it is capable of taking a share in its own being.
>   There is an original act possible to man which
> must initiate the reality of his existence. He must
> live by *willing* himself to live. . . .
>   True life *knows* and *rules* itself. The eternal life
> is life come awake.

— THE DEEPEST, DIVINEST THING IN MAN —

This is the life God offers to every man and woman.
But we must make it our own by a practical response,

by the joining, the linking, the fusing of our will with God's will.

We here encounter yet another signature MacDonald tune—the fundamental role of the will in determining God's work within us. He offers life, but we must *choose* to live. This is a far different thing than choosing to be "saved" or accepting "salvation." This is no matter of mere belief but a description of how one *lives*. In one sense, salvation has little to do with it other than placing us in relationship with a Brother-Savior to help us do what we must do, which is what he himself did—choose to live in subservience of will to the higher Will. Thus only do we take a hand in the making of ourselves, or, as MacDonald says, partake of the divine nature by taking a share in our own being.

Here at last we gain a glimpse of what MacDonald felt it was to be "made in God's image." Every one of us, in our deepest depths, shares one thing with God— the *will*. In the power to choose and make moral decisions, we are like God. Accordingly, our very separation from him remains also our single deepest point of primal contact. There alone can the bridge across the separation into oneness be built. This is where the deepest in man touches the deepest in God. The will is the remaining umbilical cord between Creator and created.

Some may misread this talk of separation, gaps, and bridges between God and man, and take offense on the basis of certain contemporary truisms about the salvationary work of Jesus, which employ similar terms and phrases. A response to such misreading is hardly worth making. I do so only because such cliché-critiques are so persistent whenever one attempts to bring fresh light into discussions of ancient truths. Therefore, I will only add this, for those fretful hearts who think MacDonald is somehow denying the work of the cross by saying that man himself has to build the bridge across the gap between himself and God: We are not here speaking of the work of the Atonement, or of Jesus at all. We are speaking of the nature of the individual operation of the will within the heart of man. We are talking about how the will functions, what it does, what it was meant to do. We are talking about which direction the will points and to whom it will give ultimate allegiance.

When a man, in *his* own will, traverses the bridge only he himself can build back into *God's* will, unity and oneness between Creator and created is reborn. The circle of life is completed.

We live by the will of the self-existent God. The links of unity with him already exist within us. All they need is to be brought together. In order to find the link in our being with which to close the circle of immortal oneness with the Father, we must of course search the deepest of man's nature. There only can it be found.

And there we do find it. For the *will* is the deepest, the strongest, the divinest thing in man. So, I presume, is it in God, for such we find it in Jesus Christ. Here, and here only, in the relation of the two wills, God's and his own, can a man come into vital contact with the All-in-all. . . . When a man can and does entirely say, *Not my will, but thine be done*—when he so wills the will of God as to do it—then is he one with God, one as a true son with a true father.

And then, having joined our will with God's, having closed, as MacDonald says, "the everlasting life-circle," how is the life of unity with our Creator sustained?

By *obedience*.

The same obedience by which Jesus lived in the will of his father.

> When a man wills that his being be conformed to that being of his origin . . . when a man thus accepts his own causing life, *and sets himself to live the will of that causing life* . . . he thus receives God's life into himself. He becomes, in the act, a partaker of the divine nature, a true son of the living God, and an heir of all he possesses. By the obedience of a son, he receives into himself the very life of the Father.
>
> Obedience is the joining of the links of the eternal round. Obedience is but the other side of the creative will. Will is God's will, obedience is man's will. The two make one. . . .
>
> If we do the will of God, eternal life is ours. . . . Our souls shall thus become vessels ever growing. And ever as they grow shall they be filled with more and more life proceeding from the Father and the Son. . . .
>
> We can never know the delight of the being or the abundance of the life he came to give us until we have it. But even now to the holy imagination it may sometimes seem too glorious . . . to think of awaking to this higher life and being filled with a wine which our souls were heretofore too weak to hold!

And he said unto all, "If any man
would come after me, let him deny
himself, and take up his cross daily,
and follow me. For whosoever would
save his life shall lose it; but whosoever
shall lose his life for my sake,
the same shall save it."

—Luke 9:23–24

Self-Denial

George MacDonald

I have often wondered whether the word of the Lord
"Take up his cross" was a phrase in use at the time.

When he first used it he had not yet told his disciples
that he would himself be crucified. I can hardly believe
that this form of execution was such a common thing
that the figure of bearing the cross had come into ordi-
nary speech.

As the Lord's idea of self-denial was new to men, so
too I think was the image in which he embodied it. Perhaps, being such a hateful thing in the eyes of the Jews,
the cross might have come to represent the worst misery
of a human being. But would they be ready to use as a
figure that which so sorely reminded them of their slavery? I do not think so.

Certainly the cross had not come to represent the
thing Jesus was now teaching, self-abnegation, which he

had but newly brought to light—nay, hardly to the light yet—only the twilight. And nothing less, it seems to me, than this complete denial of self can have suggested the terrible symbol.

— THE WORLD —

Christ is the way out and the way in.

He is the way out of slavery, conscious or unconscious, into liberty. He is the way out of the unhomeliness of things into the home we desire but do not know. He is the way from the stormy skirts of the Father's garments to the peace of his bosom.

To picture Christ aright we need not only endless figures but sometimes quite opposing figures. He is not only the door of the sheepfold but the shepherd of the sheep. He is not only the way but the leader in the way, the rock that followed, and the captain of our salvation.

We must become as little children, and Christ must be born in us. We must learn of him, and the one lesson he has to give is himself. He does first all that he wants us to do. He is first all that he wants us to be. We must not merely do as he did, we must see things as he saw them, regard them as he regarded them. We must take the will of God as the very life of our being. We must neither try to get our own way nor trouble ourselves as to what may be thought or said of us.

The world must be to us as nothing.

I would not be misunderstood if I may avoid it. When I say *the world*, I do not mean the physical world as God made and means it, still less the human hearts that live in it. Rather, I mean the world man makes by choosing the perversion of his own nature. This world exists apart from and opposed to God's world.

By *the world* I mean all ways of judging, regarding, and thinking, whether political, economical, ecclesiastical, social, or individual, which are not divine, which are not God's ways of thinking and regarding. I mean all ways of thinking which do not take God into account and do not set his will supreme as the one only law of life. I mean all ways of thinking which do not care for the truth of things but exalt the customs of society and its practices, which heed not what is right but the usage of the time.

— THE FIRST THING WE MUST LEAVE BEHIND —

From everything that is against the teaching and thinking of Jesus, from the world in the heart of the best man in it and especially from the world in his own heart, the disciple must turn to follow him. The first thing in all progress is to leave something behind. To follow him is to leave one's *self* behind: "If any man would come after me, let him deny himself."

Some seem to take this to mean that the disciple must go against his likings because they are his likings, must be unresponsive to the tendencies and directions and inclinations that are his, because they are his. They seem to think something is gained by abstinence from what is pleasant, or by the doing of what is disagreeable, and that to thwart the lower nature is in itself good.

Now I will not dare say what a man may not get good from, if the thing be done in simplicity and honesty. I believe that when for the sake of doing right a man does what may not be right, God will take care that he be shown the better way and will perhaps use his very mistake to reveal truth to him.

I will allow that the mere effort of will, arbitrary and uninformed of duty, may add to the man's power over his lower nature. But in that very nature it is *God* who must rule and not the man himself, however well he may mean. A man's rule of himself—if in the smallest opposition, however devout, to the law of God within him—may give rise to something far worse than even the unchained animal self he is seeking to subdue. By the pride of self-conquest, he is in huge danger of nourishing his demoniac self.

True victory over self is the victory of *God* in the man, not of the man alone. It is not subjugation that is enough, but subjugation by God.

In whatever man does without God, he must fail miserably—or succeed more miserably. No portion of a man can rule another portion, for God, not the man, created it, and the part is greater than the whole. In trying to produce what God does not intend, a man but falls into fresh conditions in which his lower nature may flourish. In crossing his natural inclinations—many of which are in themselves right—a man may develop a self-satisfaction which in its very nature is a root of all sin. Doing the thing God does not require of him, he puts himself in the place of God, becoming not a law but a lawgiver to himself. He becomes one who commands, not one who obeys. The diseased satisfaction which some minds feel in laying burdens on themselves is a pampering—little as they may suspect it—of the most dangerous appetite of that self which they think they are mortifying.

All the creatures of God are good, received with

thanksgiving. One of them can become evil only when it is used in relations in which a higher law forbids it, or when it is refused for the sake of self-discipline, in relations in which no higher law forbids, and God therefore allows it.

For a man to be his own schoolmaster is a right dangerous position. In such an arrangement, the pupil cannot be expected to make progress—except, indeed, in the wrong direction. To enjoy heartily and thankfully, or to do cheerfully without, when God wills we should, is the way to live in regard to things of the lower nature. These must not be confused with the things of *the world*. If anyone say this is dangerous doctrine, I answer, "The law of God is enough for me. For spiritual laws invented by man, I will have none of them. They are false and come of rebellion. God and not man is our judge."

— NOT TO THWART OR TEASE — BUT TO SACRIFICE

Verily Jesus does not tell us to thwart or tease the poor self. That was not the purpose for which God gave it to us! He tells us we must leave it altogether—yield it, deny it, refuse it, lose it. Thus only shall we save it. Thus only shall we have a share in our own being.

The self is given to us that we may sacrifice it. It is ours that we like Christ may have somewhat to offer— not that we should torment it but that we should deny it, not that we should cross it but that we should abandon it utterly. Then it can no more be vexed.

"What can this mean?" you ask. "We are not to

thwart, but to abandon? How abandon, without thwart-
ing?''

It means this:

We must refuse, abandon, deny self altogether as a
ruling, determining, or originating element in us. It is to
be no longer the regent of our action. We are no more to
think, "What should I like to do?" but "What would the
Living One have me do?"

It is not selfish to take that which God has made us
to desire. Neither are we very good to yield it. We
should only be bad not to do so when he would take it
from us. But to yield it heartily, without a struggle or
regret, is not merely to deny the Self, a thing it would
like, but to deny the Self itself, to refuse and abandon
it.

The Self is God's making—only it must be the "slave
of Christ," that the Son may make it also the free son of
the same Father. It must receive all from him. As well
as the deeper soul, it must follow him, not its own
desires. It must not be its own law. Christ must be its
law.

The time will come when the self shall be so possessed, so enlarged, so idealized by the indwelling God
who is its deeper, its deepest self, that no longer will
enforced denial of it be needful. It will have been finally
denied and refused and sent into its own obedient place.
It will have learned to receive with thankfulness and
demand nothing. It will turn no more upon its own centre or think anymore how to minister to its own good.

God's eternal denial of himself, revealed in him who
for our sakes in the flesh took up his cross daily, will
have been developed in the man. His eternal rejoicing
will be in God—and in his fellows, before whom he will

cast his glad self to be a carpet for their walk, a footstool for their rest, a stair for their climbing.

— THE CRUX OF SELF-DENIAL —
SEPARATING THE *SELF* FROM THE *WILL*

To deny oneself, then, is to act no more from the standing-ground of self, to allow no private communication, no passing influence between the *self* and the *will*, not to let the right hand know what the left hand is doing.

No grasping or seeking, no hungering of the individual, shall give motion to the will. No desire to be conscious of worthiness shall order the life. No ambition whatever shall be a motive of action. No wish to surpass another shall be allowed a moment's respite from death. No longing after the praise of men shall influence a single throb of the heart.

To deny the self is to welcome dispraise or condemnation or contempt of the community, or circle, or country, which is against the mind of the Living One. It is to allow no love or entreaty of father or mother, wife or child, friend or lover, to cause a turning aside from following him, but to forsake them all as ruling or ordering powers in life. We must do nothing to please them that would not first be pleasing to him.

Right deeds and not the judgment thereupon, true words and not what reception they may have, shall be our care. Not merely shall we not love money, or trust in it, or seek it as the business of life, but—whether we have it or do not have it—we will not think of it as a windfall from the tree of event or the cloud of circumstance, but as the gift of God.

We will draw our life—by the uplooking, acknowledging will—every moment fresh from the Living One,
the causing life, not glory in the mere consciousness of
health and being. It is God who feeds us, warms us,
quenches our thirst. The will of God will be to us all in
all. To our whole nature the life of the Father will be the
joy of the child. We will know our very understanding to
be his, know that we live and feed on him every hour in
the closest, most essential way.

We will know these things in the depth of our knowing, and such will be to deny ourselves and take God
instead.

— HOW TO BEGIN —

To try after such perspectives is to begin the denial,
to follow him who never sought his own. So must we
deny all anxieties and fears.

When young, we must not mind what the world calls
failure. As we grow old, we must not be annoyed that
we cannot remember, and must not regret what we cannot do or be miserable because we grow weak and sick.
We must not mind anything. We have to do with God
who *can*, not with ourselves where we *cannot*. We have
to do with the Will, with the Eternal Life of the Father
of our spirits, and not with the being which we could not
make, and which is his care.

He is our care. We are his. Our care is to will his will.
His care is to give us all things. This is to deny ourselves.

"Self, I do not have to consult you, but him whose
idea is the soul of you, and of which as yet you are all
unworthy. I have to do, not with you, but with the
source of you, by whom it is that any moment you exist.

He is the causing of you, not the caused you. You may be my consciousness, but you are not my being. If you were, what a poor, miserable, dingy, weak wretch I should be! But my life is hid with Christ in God, whence it came and whither it is returning. You will return with me, certainly, but as an obedient servant, not a master.

"Submit, or I will cast you from me and pray to have another consciousness given me. For God is more to me than my consciousness of myself. He is my life, you are only so much of it as my poor half-made being can grasp—as much of it as I can now know at once. Because I have fooled and spoiled you, treated you as if you were indeed my own self, you have dwindled yourself and have lessened me till I am ashamed of myself. If I were to heed what you say, I should soon be sick of you. Even now I am more and more disgusted with your paltry, mean face, which I meet at every turn. No! let me have the company of the Perfect One, not of you! He is my elder brother, the Living One! I will not make a friend of the mere shadow of my own being!

"Good-bye, Self! I deny you, and will do my best every day to leave you behind me."

— TRUE BELIEF IN JESUS —

In this regard we must not fail to see, or seeing must not forget, that when Jesus tells us we must follow him, we must come to him, we must believe in him. He speaks first and always as *the Son* of the Father. He does so in the active sense, as the obedient God, not merely as one who claims the sonship for the ground of being and so of further claim. He is the Son of the Father as the Son who obeys the Father, as the Son who came expressly and only to do the will of the Father. He is the messenger whose delight it is to do the will of him who sent him.

At the moment he says *Follow me*, he is following the Father. His face is set homeward. He would have us follow him because he is bent on the will of the Blessed. It is nothing even thus to think of him, except thus we *believe* in him—that is, so *do*.

To believe in him is to do as he does, to follow him where he goes.

We must believe in him *practically*—altogether practically, as he believed in his Father. Our belief is not in one concerning whom we have to hold something, but as one whom we have to follow out of the body of this death into life eternal. To follow him is not to take him in any way theoretically, to hold this or that theory about why he died, or wherein lay his atonement. Such things can be revealed only to those who follow him in his active being and the principle of his life—who *do as he did* and *live as he lived*.

There is no other following. He is all for the Father. We must be all for the Father too, otherwise we are not following him. To follow him is to be learning of him, to think his thoughts, to use his judgments, to see things as he saw them, to feel things as he felt them, to be hearted, souled, minded as he was—that so also we may be of the same mind with his Father.

This it is to deny self and go after him. Nothing less, even if it be working miracles and casting out devils, is to be his disciple. Busy from morning to night doing great things for him on any other road, we will but earn the reception, "I never knew you."

When he says, "Take my yoke upon you," he does

not mean a yoke which he would lay upon our shoulders. It is his *own* yoke he tells us to take, and to learn of him. It is the yoke he is *himself* carrying, the yoke his perfect Father had given him to carry. The will of the Father is the yoke he would have us take, and bear also with him. It is of this yoke that he says, *It is easy*, of this burden, *It is light*. He is not saying, "The yoke I lay upon you is easy, the burden light." What he says is, "The yoke I carry is easy, the burden on my shoulders is light." With the Garden of Gethsemane before him, with the hour and the power of darkness waiting for him, he declares his yoke easy, his burden light. There is no magnifying of himself. *He first* denies himself, and takes up his cross— then tells us to do the same. The Father magnifies the Son, not the Son himself. The Son magnifies the Father.

— THE CUNNING SELF —

We must be jealous for God against ourselves, and look well to the cunning and deceitful Self. For the Self will be ever cunning and deceitful until it is informed of God—until it is thoroughly and utterly denied, and God is to it also all in all. It will continue to try to deceive us till we have left it quite empty of our will and our regard, and God has come into it and made it—not indeed an inner sanctum, but an entryway for himself.

Until then, its very denials, its very turnings from things dear to it for the sake of Christ, will tend to foster its self-regard and generate in it a yet deeper self-worship. While it is not denied, only thwarted, we may through satisfaction with conquered difficulty, and supposed victory, minister yet more to its self-gratulation.

The Self, when it finds it cannot have honour

because of its gifts, because of the love lavished upon it, because of its conquests, and the "golden opinions bought from all sorts of people," will please itself with the thought of its abnegations, of its unselfishness, of its devotion to God, of its forsakings for his sake. It may not *call* itself but will soon *feel* itself a saint, a superior creature, looking down upon the foolish world and its ways, walking on high "above the smoke and stir of this dim spot." Yet all the time such a deceitful self is dreaming a dream of utter folly, worshiping itself with the more concentration that it has yielded the approbation of the world and dismissed the regard of others—even they are no longer necessary to its assurance of its own worths and merits!

In a thousand ways will Self delude itself, in a thousand ways befool its own slavish being. Christ sought not his own, sought not anything but the will of his father. We have to grow diamond-clear, true as the white light of the morning. Hopeless task it would be if it were not that he offers to come himself and dwell in us.

— DAILY DENIAL —

We must also note that, although the idea of the denial of self is an entire and absolute one, yet the thing has to be done *daily*. We must *keep on* denying.

It is a deeper and harder thing than any sole effort of the most Herculean will may finally effect. For indeed the *will* itself is not pure, is not free, until the Self is absolutely denied. It takes long for the water of life that flows from the well within us to permeate every outlying portion of our spiritual frame, subduing everything to itself, making it all of the one kind, until, reaching the outermost folds of our personality, the disease is at last cast out. Our bodies are then redeemed by indwelling righteousness, and the creation is delivered from the bondage of corruption into the liberty of the glory of the children of God. Every day till then we have to take up our cross. Every hour we must see that we are carrying it. A birthright may be lost for a mess of pottage, and what Satan calls a trifle must be a thing of eternal significance.

Is there not many a Christian who, having *begun* to deny himself, yet spends much strength in the vain and evil endeavour to accommodate matters between Christ and the dear Self—seeking to save that which he must certainly lose—though in an altogether different way from that in which the Master would have him lose it!

It is one thing to have the loved Self devoured of hell in hate and horror and disappointment. It is quite another to yield it to conscious possession by the Living God himself, who will raise it then, first and only to its true individuality, freedom, and life. With its cause within it, then, indeed, it shall be saved! How then should it but live!

Here is the promise to those who will leave all and follow him: *"Whosoever shall lose his life, for my sake, the same shall save it"*—or, as St. Matthew has it, *"find it."*

What speech of men or angels will serve to shadow the dimly glorious hope of the life of self denial:

To lose ourselves in the salvation of God's heart!

To be no longer any care to ourselves but know God taking divinest care of us, his own!

To be and feel just a resting-place for the divine

love—a branch of the tree of life for the dove to alight upon and fold its wings!

To be an open air of love, a thoroughfare for the thoughts of God and all holy creatures!

To know one's self by the reflex action of endless brotherly presence—yearning after nothing from any, but ever pouring out love by the natural motion of the spirit!

To revel in the hundredfold of everything good we may have had to leave for his sake—above all, in the unsought love of those who love us as we love them, circling us round, bathing us in bliss—never reached after but ever received, ever welcomed, altogether and divinely precious!

To know that God and we mean the same thing, that we are in the secret, the child's secret of existence, that we are pleasing in the eyes and to the heart of the Father!

To live nestling at his knee, climbing to his bosom, blessed in the mere and simple being which is one with God, and is the outgoing of his will, justifying the being by the very facts of the being, by its awareness of itself as bliss!

What a self is this to receive again from him for that which we left, forsook, refused! We left it paltry, low, mean. He took up the poor cinder of a consciousness, carried it back to the workshop of his spirit, made it a true thing, radiant, clear, fit for eternal companying and indwelling, and restored it to our having and holding for ever!

— IMAGERY AND REALITY —

All high things can be spoken only in figures and images. These figures, having to do with matters too high for them, cannot *fit* intellectually. They can be interpreted truly, understood aright, only by those who have the spiritual fact in themselves.

When we speak of a *man* and his *soul*, we imply a *self* and a *self*, reacting on each other. But we cannot divide ourselves in this way. The figure fits imperfectly.

It was never the design of the Lord to explain things to our understanding—nor would that in the least have helped our necessity. What we require is a means, a word, whereby to think and understand high things within ourselves. Such will true figures—for a figure may be true while far from perfect—always be to us. But the imperfection of the Lord's figures cannot lie in excess. Be sure that, in dealing with any truth, its symbol, however high, must come short of what glorious meaning the truth itself holds. It is the low stupidity of an unspiritual nature that would interpret the Lord's meaning as *less* than his symbols. The true soul sees, or will come to see, that his words, his figures, always represent *more* than they are able to present. For as the heavens are higher than the earth, so are the heavenly things higher than the earthly signs of them, no matter how good those signs may be.

— THE JOY THAT SHALL BE OURS —

There is no joy belonging to human nature, as God made it, that shall not be enhanced a hundredfold to the man or woman who gives up himself—even though, in so doing, he may seem to be yielding the very essence of life.

To yield self is to give up grasping at things in their second causes, as men call them. But such are merely

God's means. To yield self is to receive life's gifts directly from their source—to take them, seeing where they come from, and not as if they came from nowhere because no one appears presenting them. The careless soul receives the Father's gifts as if it were a way things had of dropping into his hand. He thus admits that he is a slave, dependent on chance and his own blundering endeavour. Even doing so, he is yet ever complaining, as if someone were accountable for the checks which meet him at every turn. For the good that comes to him, he gives no thanks—who is there to thank? At the disappointments that befall him he grumbles—there must be someone to blame!

He does not think to what Power it might be of consequence—nay, what power would not be worse than squandered—to sustain him after his own fashion, in his paltry, low-aimed existence! How could a God pour out his being to uphold the merest waste of his creatures? No world could ever be built or sustained on such an idea.

It is the children who shall inherit the earth. Such as will not be children cannot possess anything. The hour is coming when all that art, science, nature, and animal nature—in ennobling subjugation to the higher even as man is subject to the Father—can afford, shall be the possession, to the endless delight, of the sons and daughters of God. To him to whom he is all in all, God is able to give these things. To another he cannot give them, for he who is outside the truth of them is unable to receive them.

Assuredly we are not to love God for the sake of what he can give us. Nay, it is impossible to love him for any reason other than that he is our God, and is altogether good and beautiful. But neither may we forget what the Lord does not forget, that, in the end, when the truth is victorious, God will answer his creature in the joy of his heart.

For what is joy but the harmony of the spirit! The good Father made his children to be joyful. Only before they can enter into his joy, they must be like himself, ready to sacrifice joy to truth.

No promise of such joy is an appeal to selfishness. Every reward held out by Christ is a pure thing. Nor can such joy enter the soul except as a death to selfishness. The heaven of Christ is a loving of all, a forgetting of self, a dwelling of each in all, and all in each. Even in our nurseries, a joyful child is rarely selfish, generally righteous. It is not selfish to be joyful. What power could prevent him who sees the face of God from being joyful? That bliss is his which lies behind all other bliss, without which no other bliss could ripen or last.

The one bliss of the universe is the presence of God. It is simply God being to the man, and felt by the man as being, that which in his own nature he is—the indwelling power of his life. God must be to his creature what he is in himself. For it is by his essential being alone, that by which he exists, that he can create.

His presence is the unintermittent call and response of the Creative to the created, of the Father to the child. Where can be the selfishness in being so made happy? It may be deep selfishness to refuse to be happy. Is there selfishness in the Lord's seeing of the travail of his soul and being satisfied? Selfishness consists in taking the bliss from another. But to find one's bliss in the bliss of another is not selfishness.

Joy is not selfishness. The greater the joy thus

reaped, the further is that joy removed from selfishness. The one bliss, next to the love of God, is the love of our neighbour.

If any say, "You love because it makes you blessed," I deny it.

"We are blessed," I say, "because we love."

No one could attain to the bliss of loving his neighbour who was selfish and sought that bliss from love of himself. Love is unselfishness. Mainly we love because we cannot help it. There is no merit in it—how could there be in any love?—but neither is it selfish.

There are many who confuse righteousness with merit, and think there is nothing righteous where there is nothing meritorious. "If it makes you happy to love," they say, "where is your merit—it is only selfishness!"

"There is no merit," I reply, "yet the love that is born in us is our salvation from selfishness. It is of the very essence of righteousness." Because a thing is joyful, it does not follow that I do it for the joy of it. Yet when the joy is in others, the joy is pure. That *certain* joys should be joys is the very denial of selfishness. The man would be a demoniacally selfish man whom love itself did not make joyful.

It is selfish to enjoy in content while seeing others in deprivation. Even in the highest spiritual bliss, to sit careless of others would be selfishness, and the higher the bliss, the worse the selfishness. But surely that bliss is right altogether of which a great part consists in labour that others may share it. I do not doubt that the labour to bring others in to share with us will be a great part of our heavenly contentment and gladness. The making, the redeeming Father will find plenty of like work for his children to do.

Dull are those, little at least can they have of Christian imagination, who think that where all are good, things must be dull. It is because there is so little good yet in them that they know so little of the power or beauty of essential divine life. Let such make haste to be true. There will be interest and variety enough, not without pain, in the ministration of help to those yet wearily toiling up the heights of truth—perhaps yet unwilling to part with their miserable selves, which cherishing they are not yet worth being or capable of having.

— FORSAKING GOOD THINGS —

Some of the things a man may have to forsake in following Christ, he does not have to forsake because of what they are in themselves. Neither nature, art, science, nor fit society is of those things a man will lose in forsaking himself. They are God's. They have no part in the world of evil—the false judgments, low wishes, and unrealities that make up the conscious life of the self which has to be denied. These latter will never be restored to the man.

But in forsaking himself to do what God requires of him (his true work in the world, that is), a man may find he has to leave some of God's things—not to repudiate them, but rather for a time forsake them because they draw his mind from the absolute necessities of the true life in himself or in others. He may have to deny himself in leaving them—not as *bad* things, but as things for which there is not room until those of paramount claim have been so heeded that these will no longer impede but further them.

Then he who knows God will find that knowledge of him opening the door of his understanding to all other things. He will become able to behold everything from *within*, instead of having to search wearily into things from *without*. This principle gave to King David more understanding than all his teachers possessed. Then will the things he has had to leave be restored to him a hundredfold.

So will it be in the forsaking of friends. To forsake them for Christ is not to forsake them as evil. It is not to cease to love them, "for he that loveth not his brother whom he hath seen, how can he love God whom he hath not seen?" Rather it is not to allow their love to cast even a shadow between us and our Master. It is to be content to lose their approval, our relations with them, even their affection, where the Master says one thing and they another. It is to learn to love them in a far higher, deeper, tenderer, truer way than before. It is to love them in a way which keeps all that was genuine in the former way, and loses all that was false. We shall love *their* selves and disregard our own.

I do not forget the word of the Lord about *hating father and mother*. I have a glimpse of its meaning, but dare not attempt explaining it now. It is all against the Self—not against the father and mother.

— FORSAKING DOCTRINES —
WE HAVE BEEN TAUGHT

There is another kind of forsaking that may fall to the lot of some, and which they may find very difficult— the forsaking of such notions of God and his Christ as they were taught in their youth. These are ideas they held, and could hardly help holding, during the years when they first began to believe, but concerning which they now have begun to doubt the truth. And yet to cast them away seems like parting with every assurance of safety.

There are so-called doctrines long accepted of good people, which, how any man can love God and hold, except indeed by tightly shutting his spiritual eyes, I find it hard to understand. If a man cares more for opinion than for life, it is not worth any other man's while to persuade him to renounce the opinions he happens to entertain. He would but put other opinions in the same place of honour—a place which can *belong* to no opinion whatever. It matters nothing what such a man may or may not believe, for he is not a true man. By holding with a school he supposes to be right, he but bolsters himself up with the worst of all unbelief—opinion calling itself faith, unbelief calling itself religion.

But for him who is in earnest about the will of God, it is of endless consequence that he should think rightly of God. He cannot come close to him, cannot truly know his will, while his notion of him is in any point that of a false god. The thing shows itself absurd.

If such a man seems to himself to be giving up even his former assurance of salvation, in yielding such ideas of God as are unworthy of God, he must nonetheless, if he will be true, if he would enter into life, take up that cross also. He will come to see that he must follow *no* doctrine, be it true as word of man could state it, but the living Truth, the Master himself.

Many good souls will one day be horrified at the things they now believe of God. If they have not thought about them but given themselves to obedience, they may not have done themselves much harm as yet. But they can make little progress in the knowledge of God while, even if but passively, holding evil things true of him. If, on the other hand, they do think about them, and find in them no obstruction, they must indeed be far from anything to be called a true knowledge of God.

But there are those who find such notions a terrible obstruction, and yet imagine or at least fear them true. Such must take courage to forsake the false in *any* shape, to deny their old selves in the most seemingly sacred of prejudices, and follow Jesus, not as he is presented in the tradition of the elders but as he is presented by himself, his apostles, and the spirit of truth.

There are "traditions of men" that have come down to us after the time of Christ as well as those that existed before him. Indeed, these latter are far worse than those first-century traditions of the Pharisees in that they "make of none effect" yet higher and better things.

We have to look at such things to see and recognize *how we have learned of Christ.* Thus, *the Truth, who is the Son, will make us free.*

Insights Into
Self-Denial

MICHAEL PHILLIPS

— WRITINGS TOO FULL —

The ideas contained in the writings of George Mac-
Donald are not for the spiritually faint of heart. G. K.
Chesterton, in his 1924 Introduction to Greville Mac-
Donald's *George MacDonald and His Wife*, commenting
on MacDonald's work, said, "He wrote nothing empty;
but he wrote much that is rather too full." He was
speaking primarily of MacDonald's fantasies and fiction,
but I think the same applies to his nonfiction and didac-
tic writings.

Too full, indeed, many of his ideas are for those inter-
ested in commonplace religion—the religion of the
masses, the Christianity of Sundays alone, the so-called
faith comprised of the doctrines of "belief" rather than
the imperative *Follow me* of discipleship.

MacDonald did not write for the formula-minded. Empty religious jargon was an offense to him. He wrote for fellow pilgrims, seeking, like him, to obey the words of that timeless summons *Follow me*, wherever such obedience might lead.

We now arrive at a dividing line, a point, we might say, of no return, beyond which some may not care to go. "If MacDonald intends to strike *this* deeply into the marrow of being," these may be saying to themselves after what they have just read, "then I've had just about enough, thank you very much."

It is precisely because of that potential response that I considered saving this chapter for a later book in the *Life With God* series. I thought perhaps I might sneak it in where it would cause less annoyance and possible rejection than as one of the opening chapters of the very first volume. I did not want to turn readers away just when many might still be trying to make up their minds what they think about this plainspoken Victorian Scotsman. But the theme of *self-denial* is so pivotal and foundational to what MacDonald believed about the Christian walk that, in a sense, it *has* to shine out forcefully from the beginning. If some are offended or uncomfortable with his penetrating words, they are not going to find much in MacDonald to satisfy their spirits anyway. They may as well discover that fact sooner rather than later.

Of course, I am uncomfortable with his words too. I don't like the idea of self-denial any more than anyone else. We ought all to be a little unsettled and uncomfortable with what we have just read!

What cozy homes we each make for our nice little demon-self in out-of-the-way corners of our spiritual beings. He doesn't cause too much fuss. Out of sight in the basement, we don't let him interfere too greatly with what we are accustomed to calling our "spiritual growth."

Then along comes this MacDonald fellow, bringing giant searchlights into the place and exposing the ugly thing in my character for the demon it is!

Yes, I am uncomfortable. I am uncomfortable every time I read this probing, piercing, penetrating sermon on self-denial. I squirm and writhe and complain, as perhaps you did. But nonetheless do I recognize it as a message my world-tending, flesh-satisfying soul needs to be reminded of about every ten minutes!

Too full?

Perhaps . . . in the same way the Gospels are too full—full of more truth and wisdom than I will ever be adequately able to absorb or adequately live in my lifetime. Thus the challenge of MacDonald's words, like those of his Lord, never grow old, never grow empty, and never lose their power to move me.

— THE WORLD —

The sermon called "Self-Denial," first appearing in *Unspoken Sermons, Second Series,* follows in natural progression from the two previous chapters:

Creation comes first. *Life* emerges out of that creation. And the sustaining of that life of obedience, which has been created in Christ by the deathing of his will into the will of the Father, is accomplished through moment-by-moment *self-denial.*

These chapters thus form a threefold unity and foundation to define and describe the undergirding principles upon which our lives in Christ are based and how practically they are to be lived.

Continuously remarkable to me is how timelessly contemporary are George MacDonald's writings!

We speak a great deal in Christian circles these days about "the world." Our world is *so* different from the world in which George MacDonald wrote, that of the 1860s, 1870s, and 1880s. Just imagine how different it is! As he begins to address the pivotal subject of self-denial, however, MacDonald plunges immediately into an exposure of *the world* as the great opposing force to God's perspective. As he does so, one would hardly know that a day had gone by since the writing.

His words remind me of the many times I tried, in vain, to explain being "separated from the world" to our sons, who neither cared for the idea nor wanted my notions of it imposed upon them. How do contemporary twenty-first-century Christians who live in cities, drive cars, use credit cards, watch TV, buy the world's goods, own property, run businesses, and to all outward appearances are intimately connected with "the world" on many levels . . . what could people like *us* possibly have to do with separation from the world? No wonder I had a difficult time explaining it.

We have a good friend who is also fond of talking about separation from the world. To him, however, it means something very different than what I tried to communicate to our sons. He longs to buy forty acres as far from any population center as possible, and there, with a community of like-minded Christians, to cut himself off in all ways from economic society—producing the water supply and power, growing and raising food and everything else needful to support the community. When Jesus spoke of being *in* the world but not *of* the world, I do not believe it was this kind of disconnected lifestyle he had in mind—he was pointing to something internal and of the heart.

MacDonald clarifies the matter with both simplicity and profundity:

> We must become as little children, and Christ must be born in us. We must learn of him, and . . . see things as he saw them, regard them as he regarded them. We must take the will of God as the very life of our being. . . . The world must be to us as nothing.
>
> I would not be misunderstood if I may avoid it. When I say *the world*, I do not mean the physical world as God makes and means it. . . . By *the world* I mean all ways of judging, regarding, and thinking, whether political, economical, ecclesiastical, social, or individual, which are not divine, which are not God's ways of thinking and regarding. I mean all ways of thinking which do not take God into account and do not set his will supreme as the one only law of life. I mean all ways of thinking which do not care for the truth of things but exalt the customs of society and its practices.

Turning our backs on "the world" in this sense, learning to see and think and respond as God does, is the beginning of self-denial.

> From everything that is against the teaching and thinking of Jesus, from the world in the heart of the best man in it and especially from the world in

his own heart, the disciple must turn to follow him. The first thing in all progress is to leave something behind. To follow him is to leave one's *self* behind: "If any man would come after me, let him deny himself."

— THE PURPOSE OF INDIVIDUALITY — AND UNIQUENESS OF SELF

With MacDonald everything is upside-down. This should hardly surprise us, for is it not exactly so with MacDonald's Master? Everything in God's kingdom is precisely inverted from man's order and expectation: The last are first, the first are last, servants rule, God the infinite is like a child, to possess more give everything away, ridicule is cause to give thanks.

What kind of kingdom can it be that functions according to such parameters!

To the eyes of mankind, individuality and independence are the greatest possible possessions (besides wealth)! And as we give our individuality self-expression, as we grow independent of any and all others, our personhood expands. This is life—to be uniquely and independently and individually *ourselves*! If we can have money to go with it, so much the better. This is the ultimate freedom!

Suddenly here comes MacDonald and says, "No—that's all wrong. You've got it completely backwards. You were not given your self to grow it into a prideful and autonomous entity of its own. In truth, it is not even yours at all. You were *given* it to use, so that you would have something precious and valuable to place on the altar . . . after which, but not before, it might *become* truly yours."

> Verily Jesus does not tell us to thwart or tease the poor self. That was not the purpose for which God gave it to us! He tells us we must leave it altogether—yield it, deny it, refuse it, lose it. Thus only shall we save it. Thus only shall we have a share in our own being.
> The self is given to us that we may sacrifice it. It is ours that we like Christ may have somewhat to offer—not that we should torment it but that we should deny it . . . that we should abandon it utterly.

Then as we recover ourselves from the shock of his saying that we must give up and deny the one and only thing we thought we possessed, he explains why: To do so is the only way into life as God's sons and daughters.

> We must refuse, abandon, deny self altogether as a ruling, determining, or originating element in us. It is to be no longer the regent of our action. We are no more to think, "What should I like to do?" but "What would the Living One have me do?"

Reflect a moment on that sentence: "It is to be no longer the regent of our action."

A regent is one appointed to administer a nation or state because the actual king or queen is a minor or is incapacitated. Many of Scotland's most difficult periods of history grew out of years when a regent, or a board of regents, was in control. Mary Queen of Scots was less than a week old when she succeeded to the throne of Scotland in 1642 and became queen. Yet most of her childhood and youth was spent in France, while Scotland was controlled by regents and councils (and invaded by the English!).

I may be reading more into this passage than MacDonald intended. Perhaps he only meant to say that the self is not to rule. But I think it possible that he was thinking of the wider meaning implied by the need within us of a "regency" to govern our affairs.

We were created in the image of God to be his sons and daughters, and thus also "kings and heirs." We were each meant to rule, within the kingdom of God, over that province he has given us to command—namely, ourselves. But we are not yet mature kings and queens, we are still children. Some of us are not yet even that. We are not yet capable of ruling as the wise son-kings and daughter-queens he fashioned us to be. A regent is necessary.

But the regents God gave to help us rule during our kingly infancy—the conscience and the will—we have ousted from control. We have allowed an invasion of the province and have installed our self as regent instead.

MacDonald calls upon us to banish the usurper: *The self is to be no longer the regent of our actions.*

— THE SELF AND THE WILL —

Christians have been talking of self-denial for almost two thousand years because Jesus so clearly taught it. But how many have practically made self-denial the ruling and guiding principle of their lives?

One of our difficulties is that we simply don't understand very deeply—in a practical and moment-by-moment way—just *how* to deny ourselves as Jesus instructed. Does it mean I don't take another helping of dessert? Does it mean I don't buy the new suit I want but don't need? Does it mean I make do with a utilitarian car rather than enjoy the luxury of a nicer one? Does it mean I don't complain at unfair treatment though I dearly would like to? Does it mean I serve on the church committee though I would rather decline?

To address these and similar questions of how the thing is actually to be done, MacDonald offers one of the most brilliant, incisive, and altogether practical insights found anywhere in his writings. He separates for us the *self* and the *will*.

The *self* is the seat of our wants and desires, our fleshly and soulish inclinations.

The *will* is the seat of our decision-making power, that place within us where choices are made.

For most the two act in tandem, if not as a single entity, certainly as two conjoined components of a functioning whole. They are as two equal spatial globes, exerting exactly the same gravitational force and pull on the other and therefore inextricably linked and forever encircling round and round about each other.

In the example of the extra portion of dessert, for instance, for most the moment the *desire* is felt, the *decision* is made. I *want*, therefore I *will*. The self and will, functioning in complete harness and unity, act as a single expression of personhood. We observe, either in another or in ourselves, a *single* act—the taking of another portion. We cannot even differentiate between the two internal impulses which lead to the act.

Now, one individual may take the extra slice of pie: *I want, therefore I will.* Another may decline it. But has the latter denied himself or herself? Or has merely a different desire of the self made itself felt more strongly: "I want to lose weight, therefore I will *not* take another piece of pie."

In both cases, the decision-making equation reduces to the joint and connected operation of the self and the will: *I want, therefore I will.*

In the case of a new suit, perhaps we might say, "I want . . . but I can't afford it." So perhaps the self *is* effectively denied what it wants. But have I denied myself? Has *self-denial* taken place? No. For if money was no object, the new car or new clothes would be no different than the extra slice of pie. The fact that the self may occasionally be thwarted is not the same as self-denial. *I want, but can't* does not equal self-denial.

It is the action upon the self, in response to its inclinations and desires, that MacDonald would have us examine within ourselves—the action which *we* take upon the self. To do so, he now proceeds to turn this equation, by which humanity has functioned since time began, on its ear!

He tells us we must separate the two things. We must break the gravitational pull between the *self* and the *will.*

We must no longer allow the self and the will to function as one, he says. They must be seen as separate, because they *are* separate. They have always been separate, but we have lost sight of that separateness and allowed them to draw ever closer and closer to one another. Now we must *completely* separate them, separate them with so vast a space between them that they exert not the slightest influential pull on one another, separate them across the vastness of inner human space by millions of light-years. The planet of *self* must be removed from the solar system in which *will* functions and be sent to a far corner of the universe where no more attraction will exist between the two.

Self must be sent away, because the planet of will has linked itself to the orbit of another Sun.

What a massive reorientation this requires!

Deeply ingrained from our very infancy is the equation *I want, therefore I will*. The toddler, seeing a bright ball in front of him, does not glance to his mother to gain an indication of which direction his choice should go. He simply stretches out his hand to grasp it. *I want, therefore I will possess*. And so we continue throughout life, the same equation of thought and action guiding us all our days.

But if we hope to live as children of God, MacDonald says this equation must be recomputed. Decisions are no more to have anything to do with what the self wants or does not want.

I want issues from one portion of our personhood, that place called Self.

I will issues from another place within us that has not the slightest connection with the other.

The two do not see each other. They do not speak to one another. They exert no influence over the other. The planets have been gravitationally disconnected.

Since we cannot remove the self literally millions of light-years away from the will, at least we can begin thinking of them as separate within us, one in the brain, if you will, the other in the heart, one under the left shoulder, if you prefer, the other under the right, one in the foot, the other in the hand. However you want to conceive of it, the self and the will must be disassociated and unlinked. They must cease to have any functioning interconnection. They cannot talk to each other. The self cannot be allowed to try to persuade and convince. They must exist on opposite sides of our personal universe.

Self-denial does not mean that the *I want* of self ceases to exist, stops inserting its claims, quits wanting its own way. Many young and wrongly taught Christians idealistically assume that being "dead to sin" and living in "grace" somehow imply a lessening of the self's demands. It may, in time, change its tactics, but its goal will *always* be to retake its position of regency over the will.

No. The *I want* of self remains. But the separation which we have effected between it and the will means that we no longer listen to its voice when making decisions.

I will functions out of a different seat within us—a seat of far greater authority, dignity, and power now that it has been separated from self's influence. In this place, self is no longer allowed to voice its desires. Not only does it have no vote, it does not even have the right to advise and offer its counsel. The will is now listening to another Voice.

The new equation by which the self functions is: *I want, therefore nothing.*

The new equation for the will is: *He wants, therefore I will.*

To deny oneself, then, is to act no more from the standing-ground of self, to allow no private communication, no passing influence between the *self* and the *will*, not to let the right hand know what the left hand is doing.

No grasping or seeking, no hungering of the individual, shall give motion to the will. No desire to be conscious of worthiness shall order the life. No ambition whatever shall be a motive of action. No wish to surpass another shall be allowed a moment's respite from death. No longing after the praise of men shall influence a single throb of the heart.

— THE FIGHT! —

Will the self take this banishment and removal to the outer darkness where exists utter non-communication between it and the will, without a peep?

Not for a second.

All its life it has controlled the will. Now to be told that its influence is over, dead, past—verily will it fight back! And so we too must meet the challenge boldly and head on, confronting its whimpers and arguments and lies with fortitude and determination.

The equation for ruling the self thus becomes: *I want, therefore . . . Quiet! Away with you! You have no more say here!*

> "Self, I do not have to consult you. . . . I have to do, not with you, but with the source of you. . . . He is the causing of you. . . . You may be my consciousness, but you are not my being. If you were, what a poor, miserable, dingy, weak wretch I

should be! But my life is hid with Christ in God, whence it came and whither it is returning. You will return with me, certainly, but as an obedient servant, not a master.

"Submit, or I will cast you from me. . . . For God is more to me than my consciousness of myself. He is my life, you are only so much of it as my poor half-made being can grasp—as much of it as I can now know at once. Because I have fooled and spoiled you, treated you as if you were indeed my own self, you have dwindled yourself and have lessened me till I am ashamed of myself. If I were to heed what you say, I should soon be sick of you. Even now I am more and more disgusted with your paltry, mean face, which I meet at every turn. No! let me have the company of the Perfect One, not of you! He is my elder brother, the Living One! I will not make a friend of the mere shadow of my own being!

"Good-bye, Self! I deny you, and will do my best every day to leave you behind me."

— SHOULD AND OUGHT —

Now, for some the self/will equation rises to a higher plane. I do not mean to imply, nor do I think MacDonald would suggest, that every person on the face of the planet is *utterly* selfish in every way. Obviously there are times when we pause to consider the question: *Should* I, or *ought* I do such and such?

It would be nice to think that Christians ask this question more than others. Only God knows. But spirituality aside, the world is full of good, decent, courteous, nice people who *are* considerate of others and who *do* make unselfish choices.

Yet for most, I do not say all, even the questions of *should* and *ought* reflect back upon the individual with the perhaps unspoken or even subconscious question how it is likely to affect him or her rather than appealing to some higher standard of Should or Ought according to what *He* desires to be done.

Even the askers of should and ought listen to the voice of self speaking to the will. Theirs is just a nicer and more considerate self. The *self*, we must never forget, comes in all sizes and shapes. Some *selfs* are very nice indeed, soft-spoken, gracious, pleasant, even, as it suits them, considerate of others.

— TRUE FOLLOWING —

MacDonald never spoke in trivialities or impracticalities. If there was not something to be *done* in connection with any truth, he would expend little energy upon it.

> When Jesus tells us we must follow him . . . he speaks first and always as *the Son* of the Father. He does so in the active sense, as the obedient God. . . . He is the Son of the Father as the Son who obeys the Father. . . .
>
> At the moment he says *Follow me*, he is following the Father. . . . He would have us follow him because he is bent on the will of the Blessed. It is nothing even thus to think of him, except thus we *believe* in him—that is, so *do*.

*To believe in him is to do as he does, to follow
him where he goes.*

We must believe in him *practically*—altogether
practically, as he believed in his Father. Our belief
is not in one concerning whom we have to hold
something. . . . To follow him is not to take him in
any way theoretically. . . . Such things can be
revealed only to those . . . who *do as he did* and *live
as he lived*.

There is no other following. . . . To follow him
is to be learning of him, to think his thoughts, to
use his judgments, to see things as he saw them, to
feel things as he felt them, to be hearted, souled,
minded as he was. . . .

This it is to deny self and go after him. Nothing
less, even if it be working miracles and casting out
devils, is to be his disciple. Busy from morning to
night doing great things for him on any other road,
we will but earn the reception, "I never knew
you."

— THE SELF'S SHIFTING TACTICS —

Seeing itself losing the battle for control of the will,
and with it the control of our entire being, the self often
changes its tactics and adopts more cunning strategies.
Gradually it will begin to use the art of subtle persuasions, especially spiritual persuasions aimed to infiltrate
pride, in order to regain its foothold in the sanctuary of
the will, with the eventual objective of regaining the
will's listening ear.

We must be jealous for God against ourselves, and look well to the cunning and deceitful Self. For the Self will be ever cunning and deceitful. . . . It will continue to try to deceive us till we have left it quite empty of our will and our regard. . . .

Until then, its very denials . . . will tend to foster its self-regard and generate in it a yet deeper self-worship. While it is not denied, only thwarted, we may . . . minister yet more to its self-gratulation.

The Self, when it finds it cannot have honour because of its gifts, because of the love lavished upon it, because of its conquests . . . will please itself with the thought of its abnegations, of its unselfishness, of its devotion to God. . . . It will soon *feel* itself a saint, a superior creature. . . . Yet all the time such a deceitful self is dreaming a dream of utter folly, worshiping itself with the more concentration. . . .

In a thousand ways will Self delude itself, in a thousand ways befool its own slavish being.

But when we do deny it, a higher Self awaits us, toward which the individuality and independence of personhood we thought we had left behind was pointing all along.

The time will come when the self shall be so possessed, so enlarged, so idealized by the indwelling God who is its deeper, its deepest self, that no longer will enforced denial of it be needful. It will have been finally denied and refused and sent into its own obedient place. It will have learned to receive with thankfulness and demand nothing. It

will turn no more upon its own centre or think anymore how to minister to its own good. . . .

What a self is this to receive again from him for
that which we left, forsook, refused! We left it paltry, low, mean. He took up the poor cinder of a
consciousness, carried it back to the workshop of
his spirit, made it a true thing, radiant, clear, fit for
eternal companying and indwelling, and restored it
to our having and holding for ever!

— DENIAL OF WRONG BELIEFS —

MacDonald ends this powerful study of self-denial
on a curious yet important note. There are some, he
says, for whom one of the most vital denials of all may
be the denial of false doctrines they have been taught
about God.

Having grown up in the shadow of Scottish Calvin-
ism, where the portrayal of God was anything but the
loving, forgiving, embracing Father George MacDonald
later discovered him to be, all his life he had great sym-
pathy for those in similar circumstances—those who
were entrenched in systems of belief and whose fears
prevented the exploration of possibilities beyond the
bounds of those confining orthodoxies. But though he
was sympathetic for those whose hearts were true in
that struggle in which he had himself engaged, few
things so roused his righteous anger as those Christian
teachers, leaders, and theologians determined to keep
their flocks bound to doctrines which MacDonald considered an outrage against God's character.

Courage was required in both camps, and MacDonald regularly called for it—courage to deny doctrines

that say things of God from which the true heart recoils, and courage to speak boldly in the face of a theology that was no more than a revived tradition of the elders of Pharisaism.

There are so-called doctrines long accepted of good people, which, how any man can love God and hold, except indeed by tightly shutting his spiritual eyes, I find it hard to understand. If a man cares more for opinion than for life . . . holding with a school he supposes to be right, he but bolsters himself up with the worst of all unbelief—opinion calling itself faith, unbelief calling itself religion.

But for him who is in earnest about the will of God, it is of endless consequence that he should think rightly of God. . . . If such a man seem to himself to be giving up even his former assurance of salvation, in yielding such ideas of God as are unworthy of God, he must nonetheless, if he will be true, if he would enter into life, take up that cross also. . . .

Many good souls will one day be horrified at the things they now believe of God. . . . They can make little progress in the knowledge of God while, even if but passively, holding evil things true of him. . . .

But there are those who find such notions a terrible obstruction, and yet imagine or at least fear them true. Such must take courage to forsake the false in *any* shape, to deny their old selves in the most seemingly sacred of prejudices, and follow Jesus, not as he is presented in the tradition of the elders but as he is presented by himself, his apostles, and the spirit of truth.

The Truth shall make you free. . . .
Whosoever committeth sin, is the
servant of sin. And the servant abideth
not in the house for ever: but the Son
abideth ever. If the Son therefore shall
make you free, ye shall be free indeed.

—JOHN 8:32, 34–46

Freedom

GEORGE MACDONALD

— WHOSE SLAVES? —

As this passage about freedom in John 8 stands, I have not been able to make sense of it.

No man could be in the house of the Father by virtue of being the servant of sin. Yet the man of whom Jesus speaks is in the house as a servant, and the house in which he serves is not the house of sin but the house of the Father.

The utterance is confusing at best, and the reasoning faulty. He must be in the house of the Father on some other basis than sin.

This would be sufficient cause for leaving the passage alone, as one where perhaps the words of the Lord were misrepresented—or where, at least, perceiving more than one fundamental truth involved in the passage, I myself have failed to follow the argument. Most scriptural difficulties of similar nature have originated, I can hardly doubt, with some scribe who, desiring to explain what he did not understand, wrote his worthless gloss in the margin. The next copier took the words for an omission that ought to be replaced in the body of the text. Inserting them in his copy, he thus falsified the teaching and greatly obscured its intention. How much we owe to the critics who have searched the Scriptures and found what really was written.

In the present case, I do not see that I could ever have suggested where the corruption, if any, lay had it not been for Dr. Westcott's notation. He gives us to understand that there is another way of looking at the passage that has "a reasonable probability of being the true reading." The difference is indeed small to the eye but is great enough to give us fine gold instead of questionable ore. In seeking an alternative reading of this kind, I base my hope on what seems *logical* against what seems *illogical*, on what seems radiant against what seems trite.

What I take for the true reading, then, I render into English thus: *"Every one committing sin is a slave. But the slave does not remain in the house for ever; the son remaineth for ever. If then the Son shall make you free, you shall in reality be free."*

The King James Version gives, "Whosoever committeth sin, is the servant *of sin.*" The Revised Version of 1885 gives, "Every one that committeth sin is the bondservant *of sin.*" Both versions accept the reading that has the words *"of sin."* The statement is certainly in itself true but appears to me useless for the argument that follows.

And I think it may have been what I take to be the true reading that suggested to the apostle Paul what he says in the beginning of the fourth chapter of his epistle to the Galatians—words of spirit and life from which has been mistakenly drawn the doctrine of adoption, merest poison to the child-heart. The words of the Lord here are not that he who sins is the slave of sin—utterly true as that is—but that he is a *slave*. And the argument shows that he means a slave to *God*.

The two are perfectly consistent. No amount of slavery to sin can keep a man from being as much the slave of God as God chooses in his mercy to make him. It is his sin that makes him a slave instead of a child.

His slavery to sin is his ruin. His slavery to God is his only hope. God indeed does not love slavery. He hates it. He will have children, not slaves. But he may keep a slave in his house a long time in the hope of waking up the poor slavish nature to aspire to the sonship which belongs to him, which is his birthright.

But the slave is not to be in the house for ever. The father is not bound to keep his son a slave because the foolish child prefers it.

Whoever will not do what God desires of him is a slave whom God can compel to do it, however he may bear with him. He who, knowing this, or fearing punishment, obeys God, is still a slave, but a slave who comes within hearing of the voice of his master.

— CHILDREN WHO ARE YET SLAVES —

There are, however, far higher even than such obedient ones, who still are yet only slaves. Those to whom God is not all in all are slaves. They may not commit great sins, they may be trying to do right, but so long as they *serve* God, as they call it, from *duty*, and do not know him as their father and the joy of their being, they are slaves—good slaves it may be, but still slaves. If they did not try to do their duty, they would be bad slaves. They are by no means so slavish as those that serve from *fear*, but they are slaves. And because they are but slaves, they can fulfill no righteousness and can do no duty perfectly. They will always be striving after it wearily and in pain, knowing well that if they stop trying, they are lost. They are slaves indeed, for they would be glad to be adopted by one who is their own father!

Where then are the sons? I know none, I answer, who have become utterly and entirely sons or daughters. There may be such—God knows, I have not known them, or, knowing them, have not been myself such as to be able to recognize them. But I do know some who are *enough* sons and daughters to be at war with the slave in them, who are not content to be slaves to their father.

— SONS AND DAUGHTERS —

Nothing I have seen or known of sonship comes near the glory of the thing. But there are thousands of sons and daughters, though their number be yet only a remnant, who are siding with the father of their spirits against themselves, against all that divides them from him from whom they have come but out of whom they have never come, seeing that in him they live and move and have their being.

Such are not slaves. They are fighting along with God against the evil separation. They are breaking at the middle wall of partition. Only the rings of their fetters are left, and they are struggling to take them off. They are children—with more or less of the dying slave in them. They know it is there, and what it is, and they hate the slavery in them and are trying to slay it. The real slave is he who does not seek to be a child, who does not desire to end his slavery, who looks upon the claim of the child as presumption, who cleaves to the traditional authorized service of forms and ceremonies, and who does not know the will of him who made the seven stars and Orion, much less cares to obey it. Those are slaves who never lift up their heart to cry, "Father, what wouldst thou have me to do?" Such are continually betraying their slavery by their complaints. "Are we not justified in being angry?" they cry with Jonah. And truly, being slaves, I do not know how they are to help it.

When they are at last sons and daughters, they will no longer complain of the hardships and miseries and troubles of life. They will no longer grumble at their aches and pains, at the pinching of their poverty, at the hunger that assails them. No longer will they be indignant at their rejection by what is called society. Those who believe in their own perfect father can hardly blame him for anything they do not like. Ah, friend, it may be that you and I are slaves, but there *are* such sons and daughters as I speak of.

— SONS OR SLAVES —
ALL MUST BE ONE OR THE OTHER

The slaves of sin rarely grumble at that slavery. It is their slavery *to God* they grumble at. Of that alone they complain—of the painful messengers he sends to deliver them from their slavery both to sin and to himself.

They must be sons or slaves. They cannot rid themselves of their owner. Whether they deny God, or mock him by acknowledging and not heeding him, or treat him as an arbitrary, formal monarch, they are yet slaves. Taking no trouble to find out what truly pleases him, others do dull things in his service that he cares nothing about, or try to propitiate him by assuming with strenuous effort some yoke the Son never wore and never called on them to wear. They too are slaves, and not the less slaves that they are slaves to God. They are so thoroughly slaves that they do not care to get out of their slavery by becoming sons and daughters, by finding the good of life where alone it can or could lie.

Could a Creator make a creature whose well-being should not depend on himself? And if he could, would the creature be the greater for that?

Which, the creature he made *more* or the creature he made *less* dependent on himself, would be the greater? The slave in heart would immediately reply, with Milton's Satan, that the furthest from him who made him must be the freest, thus acknowledging his very existence a slavery. In so doing, he also acknowledges but two kinds of being—a *Creator*, and as many *slaves* as he pleases to make, whose refusal to obey is their unknown protest against their own essence. *Being* itself must, for what they call liberty, be repudiated! Creation itself, to go by their lines of life, is an injustice! God had no right to create beings less than himself. And as he could not create equal, he ought not to have created at all!

And yet they do not complain of having been created. They complain of being required to do justice. They will not obey, but, his own handiwork, seize from his work every advantage they can! They desire to be free with another kind of freedom than that with which God is free. Unknowing, they seek a more complete slavery.

There is, in truth, no midway between absolute harmony with the Father and the condition of slaves—submissive or rebellious. If the latter, their very rebellion is expressed by the strength of the Father in them. Made of divine essence, they thrust their existence in the face of their essence, their own nature.

Yet their very rebellion is in some sense but the rising in them of his spirit against their false notion of him—against the lies they hold concerning him. They do not see that, if his work, namely, they themselves, are the chief joy to themselves, much more might the life that works in them be a glory and joy to them than the work itself. For that life is nearer to them than they are to themselves. It causes them to be, and extends, without breach of relation, infinitely above and beyond them.

— THE CLOSEST OF ALL BONDS —

Nothing can come so close as that which creates. The nearest, strongest, dearest relation possible is between Creator and created. Where this is denied, the schism is the widest. Where it is acknowledged and fulfilled, the closeness is unspeakable.

But ever remains what cannot be said, and I sink defeated. The very protest of the rebel against slavery comes from the truth of God in him, which he cannot entirely cast from him. It comes of a slavery too low to love truth—a meanness that will *take* all and *acknowledge* nothing, as if his very being was a disgrace to him.

The liberty of the God that would have his creature free battles against the slavery of the creature who would cut his own stem from his root that he might call it his own and love it. Such a one rejoices in his own being instead of in the rock on which that being is built. Such a one regards his own dominion over himself—the rule of the greater by the less, inasmuch as the conscious self is less than the self—as a freedom infinitely greater than the range of the universe of God's being.

If he says, "At least I have it my own way!" I answer, "You do not know what your way is and what it is not. You know nothing of where your impulses, your desires, your tendencies, your likings come from. They may spring now from some chance, as of diseased nerves, or originate from some roar of a wandering bodiless devil, from some infant hate in your heart, from the greed or lawlessness of some ancestor you would be ashamed of if you knew him. Or they may occasionally emerge out of some far-piercing chord of a heavenly orchestra. And yet the moment they come up into your consciousness, you call all these thoughts and feelings and impulses your *own,* and glory in them!"

Two devils amusing themselves with a duet of inspiration, one at each ear, might soon make that lordly *me* you are so in love with rejoice in the freedom of willing the opposite at each alternate moment. At length they would drive you mad to find that you could not, determined as you set your mind to it, make a choice between one way and its opposite simultaneously.

— MANKIND'S CROWNING GLORY — FREEDOM TO WILL GOD'S WILL

The whole question rests and turns on the relation between Creative and created. It is a relation of which few seem to have the consciousness yet developed. But to live without the eternal creative life is an impossibility. Freedom from God can only mean an incapacity for apprehending the facts of existence and an incapability of understanding the glory of the creature who makes common cause with his Creator in his creation of him.

For what is the crowning glory of man's personhood but to will that the lovely will, which has called him into life and given him choice, should finish making him, should draw him into the circle of the creative heart? What is his joy except to recognize that he lives by no poor power of his own will but that he is one with the causing Life of his life, in closest breathing and willing, vital and claimant oneness with the Life of all life.

Such a creature knows the life of the infinite Father as the very flame of his life. He rejoices that nothing is done or will be done in the universe in which the Father will not make him entirely as much a sharer as it is possible for perfect generosity to make him.

If you think this is irreverent, that God will share all things with us, I doubt if you have seen the God manifest in Jesus.

But all will be well, for the little god with which you

poorly content yourselves will starve your soul to misery, until eventually the terror of the eternal death creeping upon you will compel you to seek a perfect father. Oh, ye hidebound Christians, the Lord is not straitened, but you are straitened in your narrow, unwilling souls! Some of you need to be shamed before yourselves. Some of you need the fire.

— HOW TO ENTER THIS FREEDOM — DO WHAT THE LORD TELLS US

But one who reads may call out, in the agony and thirst of a child waking from a dream of endless seeking and not finding, "I am bound like Lazarus in his grave-clothes! What am I to do?"

Here is the answer, drawn from this parable of our Lord. For the saying is much like a parable, teaching more than it actually says, appealing to the conscience and heart rather than to the understanding:

You are a slave. The slave has no claim on the house. Only the sons and daughters have an abiding rest in the home of their father. God cannot have only slaves about him forever. You must give up your slavery and be set free from it. That is what I am here for, says the Lord. If I make you free, you shall be free indeed. For I can make you free only by making you what you were meant to be, sons like myself. That is alone how the Son can work. But it is you who must become sons. You must will it, and I am here to help you.

It is as if he further said, *You shall have the freedom of my father's universe. Free from yourselves, you will be free of his heart. Your selves are your slavery. That is the darkness which you have loved rather than the light. You have given honour to yourselves and not to the Father. You have sought honour from men and not from the Father! Therefore, even in the house of your father, you have been but sojourning slaves. We in his family are all one. We have no party-spirit. We have no self-seeking. Join us, and you shall be free as we are free.*

But if then the poor starved child should cry, "But how, Lord?" the answer will depend on what he means by that *how*.

If he means "What plan wilt thou adopt? What is thy scheme for cutting my bonds and setting me free?" the answer may be a deepening of the darkness, a tightening of the bonds.

But if he means "Lord, what wouldst thou have me to do?" the answer will not tarry.

Surely in that case he will quickly reply, *Give yourself to me to do what I tell you, to understand what I say, to be my good, obedient little brother. Then I will wake in you the heart that my father put in you, the same kind of heart that I have. And it will grow to love the Father, altogether and absolutely as mine does, till you are ready to be torn to pieces for him. Then you will know that you are at the heart of the universe, at the heart of every secret— at the heart of the Father. Not till then will you be free. But then you will be free indeed!*

— WHAT CHRIST DIED TO SAVE US FROM —

Christ did not die to save us from suffering but from ourselves. He did not die to save us from injustice, far less from justice, but from being unjust.

He died that we might live—but live as he lives, by dying as he died, who died to himself that he might live unto God. If we do not die to ourselves, we cannot live to God. And he that does not live to God is dead. "Ye shall know the truth," the Lord says, "and the truth shall make you free. I am the truth, and you shall be free as I am free. To be free you must be sons like me. To be free you must *be* that which you have to be, that which you are created to be. To be free you must give the answer of sons to the Father who calls you. To be free you must fear nothing but evil, care for nothing but the will of the Father, hold to him in absolute confidence and infinite expectation. He alone is to be trusted."

Christ has shown us the Father not only by doing what the Father does, not only by loving his father's children even as the Father loves them, but by his perfect satisfaction with him, his joy in him, his utter obedience to him. He has shown us the Father by the absolute devotion of a perfect son. He is the Son of God because the Father and he are one, have one thought, one mind, one heart.

Upon this truth—I do not mean the dogma, but the truth itself of Jesus in relationship to his Father—hangs the universe. Upon the recognition of this truth—that is, upon their becoming thus true—hangs the freedom of the children, the redemption of their whole world.

I and the Father are one is the center-truth of the universe. And the surrounding truth of that central truth is *that they also may be one in us.*

The only free man, then, is he who is a child of the Father. He is a servant of all but can be made the slave of none. He is a son of the Lord of the universe. He is in himself, in virtue of his truth, free. He is in himself a king.

For the Son rests his entire claim to both royalty and sonship on this, that he knows the true name and true nature and is thus obediently one with his *Abba-Father*.

Insights Into
Freedom

MICHAEL PHILLIPS

— SEMANTIC CONVENTIONS —

In "Freedom," which appeared in *Unspoken Sermons, Third Series*, George MacDonald draws a distinction between *slaves* and *sons*.

This seems an appropriate place to mention an important potential stumbling block that some readers may already have encountered in MacDonald's writings—his use of masculine forms in their universal sense.

In some cases it has been one hundred thirty-five years, in others one hundred ten or one hundred twenty, since MacDonald penned the words that are the subject of our considerations in this series of writings. Political correctness as to feminist use of terms was unknown in his day. I sincerely hope and pray no one is put off by his use of *man* and *son* to indicate all of humanity in the case of the former, and the ultimate standing and status before God toward which we are all growing in the case of the latter.

To read into his words the slightest prejudice by his use of masculine terms would be to seriously misread both MacDonald and his intent. No man was more open toward women or more assured of God's equal and uniform revelation to, and work within, women and men. But MacDonald was also sufficiently a linguist and precise semanticist to use, and use accurately, the language of his day to succinctly express and represent his ideas.

The use of *man* for *mankind*, though falling from favor in modern times, is a use with which we are all well familiar. A little more difficult may be MacDonald's use of the words *son* and *sonship* to likewise indicate the universal obedient state under God's Fatherhood into which God is leading us—men and women alike. We are all becoming *sons* in a universal, genderless sense.

Now, in my own writing, I frequently use the word *childship* to express this same thought. Yet doing so is not without problems of its own. For *child* is not exactly synonymous with *son*, and the word *child* carries certain connotations antithetical to a right reception into the minds of some readers.

There is no perfect solution to this semantic dilemma which the changing mores of our culture present us. In this redactive work, I occasionally substitute "sons and daughters" for MacDonald's *sons*, or "childship" for his *sonship*, or "mankind" or "individual" for his *man*. But I only do so when I feel the result is smooth and accurately communicates MacDonald's meaning. I have not sought to do so merely for the sake of correctness. To make such an attempt in all cases would so alter the texture and feel of the writing, and load it down with artificiality, that more would be lost than gained. My job is not to make MacDonald politically or socially correct any more than to make him doctrinally correct. My job is to make his words and themes understandable. If a few women take offense at the idea that they are being made "sons" of God along with men, and do not care to make the translation in their minds to *sons and daughters,* I don't suppose I can help that. But then neither can I help certain others from taking offense when MacDonald says, "How terribly have the theologians misrepresented God," or than I can help ruffling the feathers of traditionalists with the words "Oh, ye hidebound Christians. . . . Some of you need the fire."

Men and women alike will be offended by MacDonald to the extent their hearts are not true. I will myself be offended by MacDonald to the extent *my* heart is not true. In the meantime, let us all seek to be sons (and *daughters!*) together and not let the conventions of language stumble us in that eternal pilgrimage.

— SLAVES AND SONS —

In "Freedom," then, MacDonald speaks of "slaves" and "sons" and the role each occupies in the house of the Father. He also clarifies the significant question as to whose slaves we are. Are we *God's* slaves or *sin's* slaves? In both cases, what is our role and future in relation to God?

I must admit that some MacDonald writings are not as crystalline in their meaning as others. I'm sure my own obtuseness is the cause when I don't fully "get it."

In such cases, I try to gain what insight I can without adding my own speculative uncertainties to muddy the waters further.

In this present case, I am not convinced that I fully see all MacDonald intends me to see.

We are all slaves of sin—that much is clear. We can choose to make ourselves slaves instead to God. And, having made ourselves slaves to God, God's higher intent is to turn us from slaves into sons and daughters, men and women who no longer have to obey out of the duty of a "slavish nature" but who obey in the joy of freely chosen sonship.

This is my reading of his words, which I hope approaches to some shadowy extent MacDonald's intent.

> His slavery to sin is his ruin. His slavery to God is his only hope. God indeed does not love slavery. He hates it. He will have children, not slaves. But he may keep a slave in his house a long time in the hope of waking up the poor slavish nature to aspire to the sonship which belongs to him, which is his birthright.

What has puzzled me here is that throughout his writings MacDonald speaks often of duty and obedience to God as our highest aim. Indeed, this oft-emphasized component of spirituality is one of his recurrent themes, and one in which he seems to imply that dutiful obedience is a good and high thing. Now here he seems to say that "slavish" obedience falls short of the ideal, which is the obedience of a son, an obedience given in gladness of heart.

There are, however, far higher even than such an obedient one, who still are yet only slaves. Those to whom God is not all in all are slaves. They may not commit great sins, they may be trying to do right, but so long as they *serve* God, as they call it, from *duty*, and do not know him as their father and the joy of their being, they are slaves—good slaves it may be, but still slaves. If they did not try to do their duty, they would be bad slaves. They are by no means so slavish as those that serve from *fear*, but they are slaves. And because they are but slaves, they can fulfill no righteousness and can do no duty perfectly. They will always be striving after it wearily and in pain, knowing well that if they stop trying, they are lost. They are slaves indeed, for they would be glad to be adopted by one who is their own father!

I see the distinction. Yet it seems a slightly different emphasis than appears elsewhere in MacDonald's writing. Perhaps we approach his intent in the realization that slaves *must* do as they are compelled to do, while fully mature sons are able to *choose* what the Father wants them to do. No doubt some of the *slave* and some of the *son* (or *daughter*) exists within us all. I will leave you to puzzle through this complex differentiation.

They must be sons or slaves. They cannot rid themselves of their owner. Whether they deny God, or mock him by acknowledging and not heeding him, or treat him as an arbitrary, formal monarch, they are yet slaves. Taking no trouble to find out what truly pleases him, others do dull things in his

service that he cares nothing about, or try to propitiate him by assuming with strenuous effort some
yoke the Son never wore and never called on them
to wear. They too are slaves, and not the less slaves
that they are slaves to God. They are so thoroughly
slaves that they do not care to get out of their slavery by becoming sons and daughters.

— FREEDOM TO EXERCISE THE WILL —

The point MacDonald has been driving at—is it not
the point he is always driving at!—is that God's intent is
to fashion sons and daughters who will *choose* him in the
free exercise of their wills, and thus obey him gladly
rather than merely obeying him as slaves who have no
freedom of choice in the matter.

The transition from slavery into sonship within the
children of God is a gradual one. The sonship must rise
as the slavery within us dies.

> The whole question rests and turns on the relation
> between Creative and created. . . . For what is the
> crowning glory of man's personhood but to will
> that the lovely will that has called him into life and
> given him choice, should finish making him. . . .
> What is his joy but to recognize that he lives by no
> poor power of his own will but is one with the
> causing life of his life. . . .
>
> Such a creature knows the life of the infinite
> Father as the very flame of his life. . . .
>
> Nothing I have seen or known of sonship comes
> near the glory of the thing. But there are thousands
> of sons and daughters, though their number be yet

only a remnant, who are siding with the father of their spirits against themselves. . . . Such are not slaves. They are fighting along with God against the evil separation. They are breaking at the middle wall of partition. . . . They are children—with more or less of the dying slave in them. They know it is there, and what it is, and they hate the slavery in them and are trying to slay it. The real slave is he who does not seek to be a child, who does not desire to end his slavery. . . . Those are slaves who never lift up their heart to cry, "Father, what wouldst thou have me to do?" . . .

When they are at last sons and daughters, they will no longer complain of the hardships and miseries and troubles of life. . . . Those who believe in their own perfect father can hardly blame him for anything they do not like. Ah, friend, it may be that you and I are slaves, but there *are* such sons and daughters as I speak of.

Toward this end of becoming sons and daughters, Jesus was sent to help us through the exercise of his own sonship. He says to us:

Give yourself to me to do what I tell you, to understand what I say, to be my good, obedient little brother. Then I will wake in you the heart that my father put in you, the same kind of heart that I have. And it will grow to love the Father, altogether and absolutely, as mine does, till you are ready to be torn to pieces for him. Then you will know that you are at the heart of the universe, at the heart of every secret—at the heart of the Father. Not till then will you be free. But then you will be free indeed!

He did not come to save us from hardship. He came to lead us into childship.

> Christ did not die to save us from suffering but from ourselves. He did not die to save us from injustice, far less from justice, but from being unjust.
>
> He died that we might live—but live as he lives, by dying as he died who died to himself that he might live unto God. If we do not die to ourselves, we cannot live to God. And he that does not live to God is dead. "Ye shall know the truth," the Lord says, "and the truth shall make you free." I am the truth, and you shall be free as I am free. To be free you must be sons like me. To be free you must *be* that which you have to be, that which you are created to be. To be free you must . . . care for nothing but the will of the Father, hold to him in absolute confidence and infinite expectation. He alone is to be trusted.

Then MacDonald concludes with what we might call a succinct summation of his entire perspective on life:

> Christ has shown us the Father not only by doing what the Father does, not only by loving his Father's children even as the Father loves them, but by . . . his utter obedience to him. He has shown us the Father by the absolute devotion of a perfect son. . . . Upon this truth . . . hangs the uni-

verse. Upon the recognition of this truth . . . hangs the freedom of the children, the redemption of their whole world.

I and the Father are one is the center-truth of the universe. And the surrounding truth of that central truth is *that they also may be one in us.*

The only free man, then, is he who is a child of the Father. He is a servant of all, but can be made the slave of none. He is a son of the Lord of the universe. He is in himself, in virtue of his truth, free. He is in himself a king.

Abba, Father!

GEORGE MACDONALD

The hardest, gladdest thing in all the world is to cry
Father! from a full heart. I would help whom I may to
call thus upon the Father.

— LOVE AND COURAGE TO —
QUESTION PHANTOM DOCTRINES

There are many things in all forms of the systematic
teaching of Christianity to block such an outgoing of the
heart as this most elemental human cry. With some they
render it simply impossible. The more delicate the
affections, the less easy to satisfy, the readier are they to
be dampened and discouraged, yea quite blown aside.
Even the suspicion of a cold reception is enough to par-
alyze them.

Such a cold wind blowing at the very gate of heaven—thank God, blowing *outside* the gate!—is the so-called doctrine of *adoption*.

When a heart hears—and believes, or half believes— that he or she is not the child of God by origin, from the first of its being, but may possibly be "adopted" into his family, the love of such a one sinks at once in a cold faint. Where is that heart's own father? And who is this Almighty One, as they call him, who would adopt it?

To myself, in the morning of my childhood, the evil doctrine was a mist through which the light came struggling, a cloud-phantom of repellent appearance—requiring the maturer thought and truer knowledge of later years to dissipate it. But in truth it requires neither much knowledge nor much insight to stand up against its hideousness. It needs but *love* that will not be denied, and *courage* to question the phantom.

A devout and honest skepticism on God's side, not to be put down by anything called authority, is absolutely necessary to him who would know the liberty wherewith Christ makes free. Whatever any company of good men thinks or believes is to be approached with respect. But nothing claimed or taught—be the claimers or the teachers who they may—must come between the soul of the man and the spirit of the Father. For he himself is the teacher of his children. Nay, to accept authority may be to refuse the very thing the "authority" would teach. It may remain altogether misunderstood precisely for lack of that natural process of doubt and inquiry, which we were intended to go through by him who would have us understand.

— WHO IS MY FATHER? —

As no Scripture is of private interpretation, so is there no feeling in the human heart which exists in that heart alone, which is not, in some form or degree, in every heart. Thence I conclude that many must have groaned like myself under the supposed authority of this doctrine. The refusal to look up to God as our father is the one central wrong in the whole human affair. The inability to do so is our one central misery. Whatever helps to clear away any difficulty from our recognition of the Father will more or less eliminate every difficulty in life.

"Is God then not my father?" cries the heart of the child. "Do I need to be adopted by him? Adoption! That can never satisfy me. Who is my true father? Am I not his to begin with? Is God not my very own father? Is he my father in word only—by a sort of legal contrivance? Truly, much love may lie in adoption, but if I accept it from anyone, that makes me in reality the actual off-spring of another! The adoption of God would indeed be a blessed thing if another than he had given me being! But if he gave me being, then it means no reception, but a repudiation. O *Father, am I not your child?*"

"No," they say, "but he will adopt you. He will not acknowledge you as his child, but he will *call* you his child and be a father to you."

"Alas!" cries the child, "if he is not my father, he cannot *become* my father. A father is a father from the beginning. A primary relation cannot be superinduced. The consequence might be small where earthly father-hood is concerned, but the very origin of my being— alas, if he be only a maker and not a father! Then am I only a machine, and not a child—not a man! If what you say is so, then it is false to say I was created in his image!

"It does not help if you tell me that we lost our birthright by the fall. I do not care to argue that I *personally* did not fall when Adam fell, for I have fallen many a time, and there is a shadow on my soul which I or another may call a curse. I cannot get rid of a something that always intrudes between my heart and the blue of every sky. But it avails nothing, either for my heart or their argument, to say I have fallen and been cast out. Can any repudiation, even that of God, undo the facts of an existent origin? Nor is it merely that he *made* me. By whose power do I *go on* living? When he cast me out, as you say, did I then begin to draw my being from myself—or from the devil? In *whom* do I live and move and have my being? It cannot be that I am not the creature of God."

"But *creation* is not *fatherhood*," they argue yet further.

"Perhaps," I say. "But creation in the image of God *is*. And if I am not in the image of God, how can the word of God be of any meaning to me? 'He called them gods to whom the word of God came,' says the Master himself. To be fit to receive his word implies being of his kind. No matter how his image may have been defaced in me, the thing defaced remains his image. It remains his defaced image—an image that can yet hear his word. What makes me evil and miserable is that the thing spoiled in me is the image of the Perfect. Nothing can be evil but in virtue of a good underlying substance. No, no! Nothing can convince me that I am not the child of God. If one says, 'Look at the animals—God made them, but you do not call them the children of God!' I answer, 'But I am to blame. They are not to blame! Indeed, I cling fast to my blame, for it is the seal of my childhood.' I have no argument to make on the basis of the animals, for I do not understand them. Two things only I am sure of with regard to them—that God is to them a faithful Creator, and that the sooner I put in force my claim to be a child of God, the better for them. For they too are fallen, though without blame."

"But you are evil," comes the argument of the doctrine further. "How can you be a child of the Good?"

"Just as many an evil son is the child of a good parent."

"But in him you call a good parent, there yet lay evil, and that accounts for the child being evil."

"I cannot explain. God let me be born through evil channels. But in whatever manner I may have become an unworthy child, I cannot thereby have ceased to be a child of God—his child in the way that a child must always be the child of the man of whom he comes. Is it not proof—this complaint of my heart at the word *adoption*? Is it not the spirit of the child crying out, *'Abba, Father'*?"

"Yes, but that is the spirit of adoption. The text says so."

"Away with your adoption! I could not even be adopted if I were not such as the adoption could reach—that is, of the nature of God. Much as he may love him, can a man adopt a dog? I must be of a nature for the word of God to come to. Indeed, I must be of the divine nature, of the image of God! Heartily do I grant that had I been left to myself, had God dropped me, held no communication with me, I could never have thus cried, never have cared when they told me I was not a child of

God. But he has *never* repudiated me and does not now
desire to adopt me. Why should it grieve me to be told
I am not a child of God if I am not a child of God? If
you say, 'Because you have learned to love him,' I
answer, '*Adoption* would satisfy the love of one who was
not but wants to be a child. For me, I cannot do without
a father, nor can any adoption give me one.'"

"But what is the good of all you say, if the child is
such that the father cannot take him to his heart?"

"Ah, indeed, I grant you, nothing! So long as the
child does not desire to be taken to the father's heart.
But the moment he does, then it is everything to the
child's heart that he should be indeed the child of him
after whom his soul is thirsting. However bad I may be,
I am the child of God. And therein lies my blame. Ah, I
would not lose my blame! In my blame lies my hope. It
is the pledge of what I am and what I am not. It is the
pledge of what I am meant to be, and what I shall one
day be—the child of God in spirit and in truth."

"Then do you dare to say the apostle is wrong in
what he so plainly teaches?"

"By no means," I answer. "What I do say is that our
English presentation of his teaching is very misleading.
It is not for me to judge the learned and good men who
have revised the translation of the New Testament—
with so much gain to everyone whose love of truth is
greater than his loving prejudice for accustomed form. I
can only say that I wonder what may have been their
reasons for retaining this word *adoption*."

— AN INACCURATE RENDITION —

In the New Testament the word is used only by the
apostle Paul. Liddell and Scott give the meaning as

"adoption as a son," which is a mere submission to popular theology. They give no reference except to the New Testament.

The relation of the word *huiōthesía* (υιοθεσια) to the form *thetòs* (θετοζ), which means "taken," or rather, "*placed* as one's child" is, I presume, the sole ground for the translating of it so. Usage plentiful and invariable, however, could not justify that translation here, in the face of what St. Paul elsewhere shows he means by the word.

This Greek word *might* be variously interpreted—though I can find no use of it earlier than St. Paul. But the English can mean only one thing, and that is *not* what St. Paul means. "The spirit of adoption" Luther translates "the spirit of a child." Adoption he translates *kindschaft*, or *childship*.

Of two things I am sure. First, that by *huiōthesía* St. Paul did not intend *adoption*. And second, that if the revisers had gone through what I have gone through because of the word, if they had felt it come between God and their hearts as I have felt it, they could not have allowed it to remain in their version.

Once more I say, the word used by St. Paul does not imply that God adopts children that are *not* his own, but rather that a second time he *fathers* his own. A second time they are born—this time from above. He will make himself tenfold, yea, infinitely their father. He will have them return into the very bosom whence they came . . . and left that they might learn they could live nowhere else. He will have them one with himself. It was for the sake of this that, in his Son, he died for them.

— A SPIRITUAL COMING OF AGE —

Let us look at the passage where Paul reveals his use of the word. It is in another of his epistles—that to the Galatians, in 4:1–7:

> But I say that so long as the heir is a child, he differeth nothing from a bondservant, though he is lord of all; but is under guardians and stewards until the term appointed of the father. So we also, when we were children, were held in bondage under the rudiments of the world: but when the fulness of the time came, God sent forth his Son, born of a woman, born under the law, that he might redeem them which were under the law, that we might receive the adoption of sons. And because ye are sons, God sent forth the Spirit of his Son into our hearts, crying, Abba, Father. So that thou art no longer a bondservant, but a son; and if a son, then an heir through God.

How could the revisers choose this last reading, "an heir through God," and keep the word *adoption*? From this passage it is as plain as St. Paul could make it, that by the word translated *adoption* he means the raising of a father's own child from the condition of tutelage and subjection to others—a state which he says is no better than that of a slave—to the position and rights of a son. None but a *child* could become a *son*. The idea is a spiritual coming of age. *Only when the child is a man is he really and fully a son.*

This meaning is held up in its earthly parallel. How many children of good parents—good children in the main too—never know those parents, never feel toward them as children might, until, grown up, they have left the house—until, perhaps, they are parents themselves, or are parted from them by death!

To be a child is not necessarily to be a son or daughter. The childship is the lower condition of the upward process toward the sonship. It is the soil out of which the true sonship shall grow. It is the former without which the latter would be impossible.

— SONS AND DAUGHTERS OF GOD'S SPIRIT —

No more than an earthly parent, God cannot be content to have only children. He must have sons and daughters—children of his soul, of his spirit, of his love—not merely in the sense that he loves them, or even that they love him, but in the sense that they love *like* him, love as he loves. For this he does not adopt them. He dies to give them himself, thereby to raise his own to his heart. He gives them a birth from above. They are born again out of himself and into himself—for he is the One and the All.

His children are not his real, true sons and daughters until they think like him, feel with him, judge as he judges, until they are at home with him and without fear before him because he and they mean the same thing, love the same things, seek the same ends.

For this are we created. It is the one end of our being and includes all other ends whatever.

It can come only of unbelief, and not faith, to make men believe that God has cast them off, repudiated them, said they are not, and never were, his children. Yet even in the midst of such unbelief, he has been all the time spending himself to make us the children he designed and foreordained us to be—children who would take him for their father!

He is our father all the time, for he is true. But until we respond with the truth of children, he cannot let all the father out to us. There is no place for the dove of his tenderness to alight. He is our father, but we are not his children. Because we are his children, we must become his sons and daughters. Nothing will satisfy him, or do for us, but that we be one with our father! What else could serve! How else should life ever be a good!

Because we are the sons of God, we must become the sons of God.

— BETTER THAN ANY POSSIBLE —
EARTHLY MEANING

There may be among my readers—alas for such!—to whom the word *father* brings no cheer, no dawn, in whose heart it rouses no tremble of even a vanished emotion. It is hardly likely to be their fault. For as children we seldom love up to the mark of reason. We often offend. And the conduct of some children is inexplicable to the parent who loves them. Yet if the parent has been but ordinarily kind, even the son who has grown up a worthless man will now and then feel, in his better moments, some dim reflex of childship, some faintly pleasant, some slightly sorrowful remembrance of the father around whose neck his arms had sometimes clung.

In my own childhood and boyhood my father was the refuge from all the ills of life, even sharp pain itself. Therefore I say to son or daughter who has no pleasure in the name *Father*, "You must interpret the word by all that you have missed in life. Every time a man might have been to you a refuge from the wind, a covert from the tempest, the shadow of a great rock in a weary land, that was a time when a father might have been a father indeed. Happy you are yet, if you have found man or woman such a refuge. So far have you known a shadow of the perfect, seen the back of the only man, the perfect Son of the perfect Father. All that human tenderness can give or desire in the nearness and readiness of love, all and infinitely more must be true of the perfect Father—of the maker of fatherhood, the Father of all the fathers of the earth, specially the Father of those who have specially shown a father-heart."

This Father would make to himself sons and daughters indeed. He would make such sons and daughters as shall be his sons and daughters not merely by having *come* from his heart, but by having *returned* thither—children in virtue of being such as whence they came, such as choose to be what he is.

He will have them share in his being and nature—strong wherein he cares for strength. He will have them tender and gracious as he is tender and gracious. He will have them angry where and as he is angry. Even in the small matter of power, he will have them able to do whatever his son, Jesus, could on the earth, whose was the life of the perfect man, whose works were those of perfected humanity.

Everything must at length be subject to man, as it was to *The Man*. When God can do what he will with a man, the man may do what he will with the world. He may walk on the sea like his Lord. The deadliest thing will not be able to hurt him: "He that believeth on me, the works that I do shall he do also; and greater than these shall he do."

> God, whose pleasure brought
> Man into being, stands away
> As it were, an handbreadth off, to give
> Room for the newly-made to live.

— GOD WILL NOT MAKE US SONS — WE MUST CHOOSE TO BE SONS

God has made us, but we have to be.

All things were made *through* the Word, but that which was made *in* the Word was life, and that life is the light of men. They who live by this light, that is, live as Jesus lived—namely, by obedience to the Father— have a share in their own making. The light becomes life in them. They are, in their lower way, alive with the life that was first born in Jesus and has now, through him, also been born in them. By obedience they become one with the Godhead.

"As many as received him, to them gave he power to become the sons of God." He does not *make* them the sons of God, but he gives them power to *become* the sons of God. In choosing and obeying the truth, man becomes the true son of the Father of lights.

— OTHER NEW TESTAMENT INDICATORS —

It is enough to read with understanding the passage I have quoted from his epistle to the Galatians to see that the word *adoption* does not in the least fit St. Paul's idea or suit the things he says. While we but obey the law

God has lain upon us, without knowing the heart of the Father whence comes the law, we are but slaves—not necessarily ignoble slaves, yet slaves nonetheless. But when we come to think *with* him, when the mind of the son is as the mind of the Father, when the action of the son is the same as that of the Father, then is that son *of* the Father indeed. Then is he a true son of God.

And in both passages—this from Galatians and that from St. Paul's epistle to the Romans, which I have placed at the beginning of this sermon—we find the same phrase, *Abba, Father*. This shows, if proof is needed, that he uses the word *huiōthesía* in the same sense in both. Nothing can be plainer than what that sense is.

Let us glance at the other passages in which St. Paul uses the same word. As he is the only writer of the New Testament who does use it, for all I know, he may have made it for himself. One of these uses is in the same eighth chapter of the epistle to the Romans. That one, however, I will keep to the last.

Another is in the following chapter, the fourth verse. There he speaks of the *huiōthesía*, literally the *son-placing* (that is, the placing of sons in the true place of sons), as belonging to the Jews. On this I have but to remark that "whose is the *huiōthesía*" cannot mean either that they had already received it or that it belonged to the Jews more than to the Gentiles. It can only mean that, as the elder brother-nation, they had a foremost claim to it. They would naturally be the first to receive it, and, in their best men, had always been nearest to it. It must be brought to fruition first in those who had received the preparation necessary to receive it. Such were the Jews. And of the Jews, such was the

Son, who brought the *huiōthesía*, the sonship, to all.

Therefore to the Jew belonged the *huiōthesía*, just as theirs was the gospel. It was to the Jew first, then to the Gentile—though many a Gentile would have it before many a Jew. Those and only those who out of a true heart cry *"Abba, Father,"* be they of what paltry little so-called church, other than the body of Christ, they may, or of no other at all, are the sons and daughters of God.

St. Paul uses the word also in his epistle to the Ephesians, the first chapter, the fifth verse. "Having predestinated us unto the adoption of children by Jesus Christ to himself," says the Authorized Version; "Having foreordained us unto adoption as sons through Jesus Christ unto himself," says the Revised. I see little difference between them—neither gives the meaning of St. Paul. If there is anything gained by the addition of the words *of children* in the one case, and *as sons* in the other, to translate the word for which "adoption" alone is made to serve in the other passages, the advantage is only to the minus-side, to that of the *wrong* interpretation.

Children we were. True sons we could never be, except through the Son. He brothers us. He takes us to the knees of the Father, beholding whose face we grow sons indeed. Never could we have known the heart of the Father, never felt it possible to love him as sons, except for him who cast himself into the gulf that yawned between us.

In and through him we were foreordained to the sonship. Even had we never sinned, we could never reach sonship without him. We should have been little children loving the Father indeed, but children far from the sonhood that understands and adores.

"For as many as are led by the spirit of God, these are sons of God."

"If any man hath not the spirit of Christ, he is none of his."

Indeed, if we have not each other's spirits, we do not belong to each other. There is no unity but having the same spirit. There is but one spirit, that of truth.

— ST. PAUL'S LARGE MEANING —

It remains to note yet one more passage.

Never in anything he wrote was it St. Paul's intention to contribute toward a system of theology. This is easy enough to show. One sign of the fact is that he does not hesitate to use this word he has perhaps himself made up, in different, and apparently opposing, though by no means contradictory, senses.

St. Paul's meanings always enliven one another. His ideas are so large that they tax his utterance and make him strain the use of words. But there is no danger to the honest heart, which alone he regards, of misunderstanding them, though "the ignorant and unsteadfast wrest them" yet. At one time he speaks of the sonship as being the possession of the Israelite, at another as his who has learned to cry *Abba, Father*. And here, in the passage I have now last to consider, that from the eighteenth to the twenty-fifth verse of this same eighth chapter of his epistle to the Romans, he speaks of the *huiōthesía* as yet to come—and as if it had to do not with our *spiritual* but our *bodily* condition. This use of the word, however, though not the same use as we find anywhere else, is nevertheless entirely consistent with his other uses of it.

The twenty-third verse says, "And not only so, but ourselves also, which have the first fruits of the spirit, even we ourselves groan within ourselves, waiting for adoption, the redemption of our body."

It is not difficult to discern that the ideas in this and his main use are necessarily associated and more than consistent. The putting of a son into his true, his fore-ordained place, has outward relations as well as inward reality. The outward depends on the inward. It arises from it and reveals it. When the child whose condition under former tutors has passed away, takes his position as a son, he naturally changes his dress and modes of life. When God's children cease to be slaves doing right from law and duty, and become his sons doing right from the essential love of God and their neighbour, they too must change the garments of their slavery for the robes of liberty. They will then lay aside the body of this death and appear in bodies like that of Christ, with whom they inherit of the Father.

But many children who have learned to cry *Abba, Father,* are yet far from the liberty of the sons of God. Sons they are and no longer children, yet they groan as being still in bondage!

Plainly the apostle has no thought of working out a theological doctrine. With burning heart he is writing a letter. Nevertheless, he gives lines plentifully sufficient for us to work out his idea. And this is how it takes clear shape:

We are the sons of God the moment we lift up our hearts, seeking to be sons—the moment we begin to cry *Father.* But as the world must be redeemed in a few men to begin with, so the soul is redeemed in a few of its thoughts and wants and ways to begin with. It takes a long time to finish the new creation of this redemption. Shall it have taken millions of years to bring the world up to the point where a few of its inhabitants shall desire God, and then shall the creature of this new birth be perfected in a day? The divine process may indeed now go on with tenfold rapidity, for the new factor of man's fellow-working, for the sake of which the whole previous array of means and forces existed, is now developed. But its end is yet far below the horizon of man's vision.

The apostle speaks at one time of the thing as to come, at another time as finished—when because of our ways of thought it is but begun. A man's heart may leap for joy the moment when, amidst the sea-waves, a strong hand has laid hold of the hair of his head. He may cry aloud, "I am saved." And indeed, he may be safe. But he is not yet saved. This is far from a sufficient salvation. So are we sons even when we begin to cry *Father*. But we are far from perfected sons. So long as there is in us the least taint of distrust, the least lingering of hate or fear, we have not fully received the sonship. We do not yet have such life in us as raised the body of Jesus. We have not yet attained to the resurrection of the dead—by which word, in his epistle to the Philippians (3:2), St. Paul means, I think, the same thing as here he means by the sonship which he puts in apposition with the redemption of the body.

Until our outward condition is that of full royal and divine sons, so long as the garments of our souls, these mortal bodies, are mean and torn and dragged and stained, so long as we groan under sickness and weakness and weariness and old age and forgetfulness and all things heavy to bear . . . so long as we have not yet received the sonship in full. So long as all these conditions remain in us, we are but getting ready one day to creep from our chrysalides and spread the great heaven-storming wings of the psyches of God.

We groan being burdened. We groan as we wait for the sonship—which is the redemption of the body, the uplifting of the body to be a fit house and revelation of the indwelling spirit, and even more, to be like that of Christ, a fit temple and revelation of *the deeper indwelling God.*

For we shall always need bodies to manifest and reveal us to each other—bodies, then, that fit the soul with absolute truth of presentment and revelation. Hence the revealing of the sons of God, spoken of in the nineteenth verse, is the same thing as the redemption of the body. The body is redeemed when it is made fit for the sons of God. Then it becomes a revelation of them—the thing it was meant for, and always, more or less imperfectly, was. Such it shall be when truth is strong enough in the sons of God to make it such, for it is the soul that makes the body. When we are the sons of God in heart and soul, then shall we be the sons of God in body too: "We shall be like him, for we shall see him as he is."

I care little to speculate on the nature of this redeemed body. I will say only two things as necessary to be believed about it. First, it will be a body that will reveal the same self as before. But, second, it will be a body to reveal the being *truly*—without the defects and imperfections of the former bodily revelation. Even through their corporeal presence we shall then know our own infinitely better, and find in them endlessly more delight, than before. These things we must believe or else distrust the Father of our spirits. Till this redemption of the body arrives, the *huiōthesía* is not fully accomplished, it is only upon the way. Nor can it come but by our working out the salvation he is working in us.

This redemption of the body—its deliverance from all that is amiss, awry, unfinished, weak, worn out, all that prevents the revelation of the sons of God, is called by the apostle, not certainly the "adoption," but the *huiōthesía, the sonship in full manifestation.* It is the slave yet left in the sons and daughters of God that has betrayed them into even permitting the word *adoption* to mislead them!

— THE POTENT OUTSHINING OF SONS —

To see how the whole utterance hangs together, read from the eighteenth verse to the twenty-fifth, especially noticing the nineteenth: "For the earnest expectation of the creation waiteth for the revealing (*the outshining*) of the sons of God." When the sons of God show as they are, taking, with the character, the appearance and the place that belong to their sonship, when the sons of God sit with *the* Son of God on the throne of their father, then shall they be in potency of fact the lords of the lower creation, the bestowers of liberty and peace upon it. Then shall the creation, subjected to vanity for their sakes, find its freedom in their freedom, its gladness in their sonship. The animals will glory to serve them, will joy to come to them for help.

Let the heartless scoff, the unjust despise! The heart that cries *Abba, Father,* cries to the God of the sparrow and the oxen. Nor can hope go too far in hoping what that God will do for the creation that now groans and travails in pain because our higher birth is delayed. Shall not the judge of all the earth do right? Shall my heart be more compassionate than his?

If to any reader my interpretation be unsatisfactory, I pray him not to spend his strength in disputing my faith but in making sure of his own progress on the way to freedom and sonship.

Only to the child of God is true judgment possible. Were it otherwise, what would it avail to prove this one or that right or wrong? Right opinion on questions the most momentous will deliver no man. Cure for any ill in me or about me there is none but to become the son of God I was born to be. Until such I am, until Christ is born in me, until I am revealed a son of God, pain and trouble will endure—and God grant they may!

Call this presumption, and I can only widen my assertion—until you yourself are the son of God you were born to be, you will never find life a good thing. If I presume for myself, I presume for you also.

But I do not presume. Thus have both Jesus Christ and his love-slave Paul represented God—as a Father perfect in love, grand in self-forgetfulness, supreme in righteousness, devoted to the lives he has uttered. I will not believe less of the Father than I can conceive of glory after the lines he has given me, after the radiation of his glory in the face of his Son. He is the express image of the Father, by which we, his imperfect images, are to read and understand him. Imperfect, we have yet perfection enough to discover our way toward the perfect.

— WHAT GLORY SHALL BE WHEN — ALL CREATION KNOWS ITS FATHER

It comes to this then, after the grand theory of the apostle:

The world exists for our education. It is the nursery of God's children served by troubled slaves, troubled because the children are themselves slaves—children but not good children. Beyond its own will or knowledge, the whole creation works for the development of the children of God into the sons of God.

When at last the children have arisen and gone to their Father, when they are clothed in the best robe with a ring on their hands and shoes on their feet, when they are shining out at length in their natural and predestined sonship, then shall the mountains and the hills break forth before them into singing. Then shall all the trees of the field clap their hands. Then shall the wolf dwell with the lamb, and the leopard lie down with the kid and the calf, and the young lion and the fatling together, and a little child shall lead them. Then shall the fables of a golden age, which faith invented, and unbelief threw into the past, unfold their essential reality, and the tale of paradise prove itself a truth by becoming a fact.

Then shall every ideal reveal itself a necessity, all aspiration although satisfied put forth yet longer wings, and the hunger after righteousness know itself blessed, because *truth is at last revealed in its fullness, not as the opinion of any man, but as the Truth that is God himself.*

Insights Into

Abba, Father!

MICHAEL PHILLIPS

— NO ADOPTION, BUT TRUE SONSHIP —

In "Abba, Father!" published in *Unspoken Sermons, Second Series,* in one sense we approach the high-water mark of George MacDonald's theology—the intimacy between the Fatherhood of God and the sonship of believers. And yet this selection does not offer us quite as much in the way of an inside glimpse into MacDonald's image of the eternal Fatherhood and the intimacy with that Fatherhood suggested by the word *Abba,* as the title might lead us to expect. The title, indeed, does not communicate particularly well what is the dominant theme MacDonald here examines—the doctrine of adoption.

There is no need to reiterate MacDonald's progression of thought as he moves through the scriptural texts to dismantle the traditionally accepted meaning of that doctrine. It is enough for our purposes here that we get his final point—that *adoption*, as commonly understood, was not in Paul's mind as he coined the word generally translated such. To MacDonald, longing to know God as his *true* Father, not merely an *adoptive* one, the suggestion of adoption was repellant. He had apparently struggled with the idea of it most of his life. He wanted to know whether he was an adopted child or a true *son*.

> To myself, in the morning of my childhood, the evil doctrine was a mist through which the light came struggling, a cloud-phantom of repellent appearance—requiring the maturer thought and truer knowledge of later years to dissipate it. But in truth it requires neither much knowledge nor much insight to stand up against its hideousness. It needs but *love* that will not be denied and *courage* to question the phantom. . . .
>
> The refusal to look up to God as our father is the one central wrong in the whole human affair. The inability to do so is our one central misery. Whatever helps to clear away any difficulty from our recognition of the Father will more or less eliminate every difficulty in life.

Instead of adoption, MacDonald sees that we are called to what he terms the coming of age of spiritual sonship:

> The idea is a spiritual coming of age. *Only when the child is a man is he really and fully a son.*
> This meaning is held up in its earthly parallel.

How many children of good parents . . . never
know those parents, never feel toward them as
children might, until, grown up, they have left the
house—until, perhaps, they are parents themselves, or are parted from them by death!

To be a child is not necessarily to be a son or
daughter. The childship is the lower condition of
the upward process toward the sonship. It is the
soil out of which the true sonship shall grow. . . .
For this he does not adopt them. He dies to give
them himself, thereby to raise his own to his heart.
He gives them a birth from above.

One of MacDonald's trademarks is the use of seemingly similar (or even identical) terms in contradistinc-
tion to one another—juxtaposing them as opposites in
order to convey to us his meaning. He employs this
technique throughout his writing with many words and
phrases.

Obviously the word *children* means "sons and daughters." They are exactly synonymous. Yet MacDonald
often juxtaposes them in order to imbue them with distinct meanings. His purpose is to clarify in our minds the
childness of the *flesh* (which may be the state in which
many Christians function, as well as non-Christians) and
that of the *spirit*. It is the distinction between that
which we cannot help and that which we choose in a
moment-by-moment way. We *are* God's children,
because he has created us, but we must *choose* to rise
into the higher childship or sonship which takes upon
itself his will for our own. To convey this, MacDonald
says,

We *are* God's children, but we must *become* his sons and daughters. . . . No more than an earthly parent, God cannot be content to have only children. He must have sons and daughters—children of his soul, of his spirit, of his love—not merely in the sense that he loves them, or even that they love him, but in the sense that they love *like* him, love as he loves.

He occasionally goes even further in this juxtaposition of sameness to convey a distinction, as when he says: "Because we are the sons of God, we must become the sons of God."

His children are not his real, true sons and daughters until they think like him, feel with him, judge as he judges, until they are at home with him and without fear before him because he and they mean the same thing, love the same things, seek the same ends.

For this are we created. It is the one end of our being and includes all other ends whatever. . . . He is our father all the time. . . . But until we respond with the truth of children, he cannot let all the father out to us. There is no place for the dove of his tenderness to alight. He is our father, but we are not his children. Because we are his children, we must become his sons and daughters. Nothing will satisfy him, or do for us, but that we be one with our father! What else could serve! How else should life ever be a good!

Because we are the sons of God, we must become the sons of God.

MacDonald's use of similarities to convey differences is here more pronounced in that he is attempting to convey clearly into our minds the distinction between adoption and fatherhood—between an unreal, pretend, false fatherhood, and the *true* Fatherhood. Thus he says, just as there is a false and a true fatherhood, there is a *fleshly childship* and a *spiritual sonship*, the one we cannot help, the other we must choose.

— IMPERFECT VESSELS —

Then MacDonald changes themes. He begins speaking to the heart, calling upon us to approach God's Fatherhood through the imagination, to imagine the *best* of all possible Fatherhoods, far better than our broken, shattered, painful, incomplete earthly images. All earthly fatherhood is broken. It does not match the ideal it was created to reflect and portray. In one of my own books I referred to earthly fatherhood as a "broken mirror." When speaking on MacDonald, my talk about God's use of earthly fatherhood to portray his heavenly Fatherhood is entitled "Imperfect Vessels."

As a young father my own hope and dream and deepest heart's desire was to be for my own sons a true and loving representation of God. I knew, of course, that such an effort would be incomplete and flawed. But despite what I recognized as my imperfection, I prayed for twenty years that God would nevertheless make fatherhood a wonderful reality in the lives and hearts of my sons. I devoted myself to that heart's desire with more energy and time and patience and sacrifice and tears and longsuffering and prayer than I did anything else in my life for those twenty years.

And now, years later, it is with *extreme* grief and tears of *heart-wrenching* sorrow that I realize that I did not convey God's fatherhood to my sons as I had hoped and prayed and honestly tried to do. Though I tried with every fiber of my being to reflect God's nature to my sons, I am but a broken vessel through which God might reflect such high truth. My grief for my own weakness and failings before my sons is with me daily.

I make this personal digression because I believe the principle involved is so very important for every one of us who would know God as he truly is. For is not my own experience one that most of humanity shares? I recently received a letter from a woman who said, "My own father was the man most like Jesus of anyone I have ever known." What a wonderful testimony. Sadly, however, her words are rare. Not many men and women would say such a thing. Certainly my sons who wrote have never said it of me. And this is representative of much of the human equation. Love is incomplete wherever we look. Love is incomplete on all sides of every relational fence. Fathers and mothers do not love very well, and sons and daughters mistake what love exists for unlove, and in their immaturity and rebellion do not love very well in return.

Love everywhere has broken down. We are imperfect vessels. The human mirror of fatherhood and motherhood is cracked and its images of God's character are blurred, distorted, and vastly incomplete. If my heart aches for the broken love between myself and two others whose lives came from mine, imagine how the heart of God is breaking from the rejection of his far greater love by an entire race whom he created!

Yet MacDonald calls upon us to look beyond the broken and failed earthly images, there to imagine a *perfect* Fatherhood.

> Therefore I say to son or daughter who has no plea-sure in the name *Father,* "You must interpret the word by all that you have missed in life. Every time a man might have been to you a refuge from the wind, a covert from the tempest, the shadow of a great rock in a weary land, that was a time when a father might have been a father indeed. . . . All that human tenderness can give or desire in the near-ness and readiness of love, all and infinitely more must be true of the perfect Father—of the maker of fatherhood, the Father of all the fathers of the earth, specially the Father of those who have spe-cially shown a father-heart."

He challenges us to recognize God's perfect love as coming from our *Father,* in spite of the fact that all earthly fathers have *not* loved to such a high purpose.

> This Father would make to himself sons and daugh-ters indeed. He would make such sons and daugh-ters as shall be his sons and daughters not merely by having *come* from his heart, but by having *returned* thither—children in virtue of being such as whence they came, such as choose to be what he is.

Then comes the theme again. We must choose to step into this higher childship under God's Fatherhood in which we have not been fully able to walk in our earthly relationships.

God has made us, but we have to be.

All things were made *through* the Word, but that which was made *in* the Word was life, and that life is the light of men. They who live by this light, that is, live as Jesus lived—namely, by obedience to the Father—have a share in their own making. The light becomes life in them. They are, in their lower way, alive with the life that was first born in Jesus and has now, through him, also been born in them. By obedience they become one with the God-head. . . .

Children we were. True sons we could never be, except through the Son. He brothers us. He takes us to the knees of the Father, beholding whose face we grow into sons indeed.

— SONSHIP TAKES TIME —

Returning to the point he made in the previous chapter ("Freedom"), MacDonald again hints at the distinction between slaves and sons, paralleling the adoptive and the true childship, and says that it takes time for full and free sonship to be developed within us. He speaks of the soul having to be redeemed and conquered by sonship a little at a time.

In conveying this idea, I find intriguing his mention of "millions of years" to describe God's work in the world. A contemporary of Darwin, and a scientist himself, MacDonald was certainly well familiar with the debate raging during his lifetime concerning origins. And while he categorically rejected any "random" or chance foundation of the physical universe and the myriad life forms found within it, we see here and in other places in his writings that he had clearly rejected the six-thou-sand-year-old-earth hypothesis in favor of an "old earth" view. Here he draws the parallel between God's long, slow redemptive work in the universe with the long, slow work of sonship that takes place within the heart of each son and daughter who looks up to call him *Father*.

> We are the sons of God the moment we lift up our hearts, seeking to be sons—the moment we begin to cry *Father*. But as the world must be redeemed in a few men to begin with, so the soul is redeemed in a few of its thoughts and wants and ways to begin with. It takes a long time to finish the new creation of this redemption. Shall it have taken millions of years to bring the world up to the point where a few of its inhabitants shall desire God, and then shall the creature of this new birth be per-fected in a day? The divine process may indeed now go on with tenfold rapidity, for the new factor of man's fellow-working . . . is now developed. . . .
>
> We groan, being burdened. We groan as we wait for the sonship—which is the redemption of the body, the uplifting of the body to be a fit house and revelation of the indwelling spirit, and even more, to be like that of Christ, a fit temple and revelation of *the deeper indwelling God*.

MacDonald then touches briefly on what will be con-sidered in more detail in "The God of the Living," so we will reserve comment on the resurrection of the body until then.

Suffice it to note once more—now on the basis of

the distinction between the present earthly body and the eternal resurrection body—MacDonald's conviction that the word usually translated *adoption* should in fact be read as "coming of age." Spiritual sonship, the redemption of the body, and broken earthly fatherhood are all incomplete here and now. But they will *come of age* there—when they are fulfilled, perfected, glorified. Then will the Fatherhood, the sonship, and the redemption be fully manifest.

> Till this redemption of the body arrives, the *huiōthesía* is not fully accomplished, it is only upon the way. Nor can it come but by our working out the salvation he is working in us.
>
> This redemption of the body—its deliverance from all that is amiss, awry, unfinished, weak, worn out, all that prevents the revelation of the sons of God, is called by the apostle . . . *the sonship in full manifestation.* . . .
>
> The world exists for our education. It is the nursery of God's children. . . . Beyond its own will or knowledge, the whole creation works for the development of the children of God into the sons of God.
>
> When at last the children have arisen and gone to their Father, when they are clothed in the best robe with a ring on their hands and shoes on their feet, when they are shining out at length in their natural and predestined sonship, then shall the mountains and the hills break forth before them into singing. Then shall all the trees of the field clap their hands. Then shall the wolf dwell with the lamb, and the leopard lie down with the kid and

the calf, and the young lion and the fatling together, and a little child shall lead them. Then shall the fables of a golden age ... unfold their essential reality, and the tale of paradise prove itself a truth by becoming a fact.

Let us therefore, as many as be perfect,
be thus minded; and if in anything ye
be otherwise minded, God shall reveal
even this unto you. Nevertheless,
whereto we have already attained,
let us walk by that same.

—PHILIPPIANS 3:15–16

Opinion and Truth

GEORGE MACDONALD

This is the reading of the oldest manuscripts. The rest of this verse is pretty clearly an unwise marginal gloss that has crept into the text.

— TRUTH AND ITS LOWER FORMS —

In its origin, *opinion* is the intellectual body of *truth*. It is that which is used for utterance and presentation by something necessarily larger than the means by which any intellect has the capacity to embody it. To the man himself, therefore, in whose mind it arises, an opinion will always represent and recall the spirit, or the truth, whose form it is—so long, at least, as the man remains true to his better self.

Hence, a man's opinion may be for him invaluable, the needle of his moral compass, always pointing to the truth from which it comes. Nor is the man's opinion of the less value to him that it may change. Indeed, to be of true value, it must have in it not only the possibility but the *necessity* of change. In every man who is alive with that life which, in the New Testament, is alone treated as life at all, opinion *must* change. For if a man's opinion is not in the process of growth, it must be dead, valueless, hurtful.

Opinion is the offspring of that which is itself born to grow. Being imperfect, it must grow or die. Where opinion is growing, its imperfections, however many and serious, will do but little hurt. Where it is not growing, these imperfections will further the decay and corruption which must already have lain hold of the heart of the man.

But it is plain in the world's history that what was once the embodiment in intellectual form of the highest and deepest of which it was then spiritually capable, has often and speedily become the source of the most frightful outrages upon humanity. How can this be?

Because it has passed from the mind in which those high thoughts grew, into other minds in which they did not grow. In the process, the original ideas of necessity altered their nature. Ideas that sprung from what was deepest in one man cast seeds which took root only in the intellectual understanding of his neighbour. These then, springing up, produced flowers indeed which looked much the same to the eye, but fruit which was poison and bitterness. And the worst result arising of all was the false and arrogant notion that it is one's duty to force one's opinion upon the acceptance of others.

Such men themselves hold with poor grasp the truth underlying the forms of their opinions. They are, in their

self-sufficiency, so ambitious of propagating the *forms*
that they actually make of themselves the worst enemies
of the *truth* of which they fancy themselves the champions.

— SECONDHAND OPINIONS —

How truly, in the case of all genuine teachers of men,
shall a man's foes be they of his own household! For of
all the destroyers of the truth which any man has
preached, none have done so effectually or so grievously
as his own followers. So many of them have received but
the *forms* and know nothing of the *truth* which gave him
those forms! They lay hold but of the nonessential, the
specially perishing in those forms. These outer aspects
of truth, doubly false and misleading in their crumbling
disjunction, proceed to force upon the attention and
reception of others, calling that the "truth" which is at
best but the bedraggled and useless fringe of its earth-
made garment.

Opinions so held belong to the theology of hell. They
are not necessarily altogether false in form, but they are
utterly false in heart and spirit.

The opinion that is hurtful is not that which is
formed in the depths and from the honest necessities of
a man's own nature, but that which he has taken up secondhand, the study of which has pleased his intellect.
Such secondhand opinions have perhaps subdued fears
and mollified distresses which ought rather to have
grown and increased until they had driven their holder
to the true physician. Some of them have puffed him up
with a sense of superiority as false as it is foolish, placing
in his hand a club with which to intellectually subjugate

his neighbor to his spiritual dictation.

Even the true man, who aims at the perpetuation of his opinion, is obstructing rather than aiding the course of that truth for the love of which he holds his opinion in the first place. *For truth is a living thing, opinion is a dead thing, and transmitted opinion a deadening thing.*

— PAUL'S FAITH: PERFECTION OF DEDICATION —

Let us look at St. Paul's feeling in this regard. And in order that we may grasp its force, let us note first the nature of the truth which he had just been presenting to his disciples, when he follows it with the words of my text (Philippians 3:7–14):

> But what things were gain to me, those I counted loss for Christ.
>
> Yea, doubtless, and I count all things but loss for the excellency of the knowledge of Christ Jesus my Lord: for whom I have suffered the loss of all things, and do count them but dung, that I may win Christ,
>
> And be found in him, not having mine own righteousness, which is of the law, but that which is through the faith of Christ, the righteousness which is of God by faith:
>
> That I may know him, and the power of his resurrection, and the fellowship of his sufferings, being made conformable unto his death;
>
> If by any means I might attain unto the resurrection of the dead.
>
> Not as though I had already attained, either were already perfect: but I follow after, if that I

may apprehend that for which also I am appre-
hended of Christ Jesus.

Brethren, I count not myself to have appre-
hended: but this one thing I do, forgetting those
things which are behind, and reaching forth unto
those things which are before,

I press toward the mark for the prize of the
high calling of God in Christ Jesus.

St. Paul is declaring to the Philippians the idea upon
which, so far as it lay with him, his life was constructed.
This was the thing for which he lived, to which the
whole conscious effort of his being was directed—
namely, to be in his very nature one with Christ, to
become righteous as he is righteous. It was his desire to
die into Christ's death, so that he himself should no
more hold the slightest personal relation to evil, but be
alive in every fiber of his being to all that is pure, lovely,
beautiful, perfect. He had been telling them that he
spent himself in continuous effort to lay hold upon that
for the sake of which Christ had laid hold on him. This
he declares the sole thing worth living for. It is the hope
of this—the hope of becoming one with the living
God—which keeps a glorious consciousness awake in
him, amidst all the unrest of a being not yet at harmony
with itself, and a laborious and persecuted life.

He cannot therefore be indifferent to the truth to
which he has borne this witness, when he adds, "If in
anything ye be otherwise minded." It is to him even the
test of perfection, whether his readers be thus minded
or not. For although a moment before he has declared
himself short of the desired perfection, he now says,
"Let as many of us as are perfect be thus minded."

— OPINION, THE CLOAK OF BELIEF —

There is no room here for that unprofitable thing, bare logic. We must look through the shifting rainbow of his words, gather all their tints together, then turn our backs upon the rainbow that we may see the glorious light which is the soul of it. St. Paul is not yet the man he would be, which he must be. But he, and all they who with him believe that the perfection of Christ is the sole worthy effort of a man's life, are in the region, though not yet at the centre, of perfection. They are, even now, not indeed grasping but in the grasp of that perfection. He tells them this is the one thing to mind, the one thing to go on desiring and laboring for with all the earnestness of a God-born existence.

But if anyone be at all otherwise minded—that is, of a different opinion—what then? Is it of no consequence? No, verily—it is of *such* consequence that God will himself unveil to them the truth of the matter.

This is Paul's faith, not his opinion. Faith is that by which a man lives *inwardly* and orders his way *outwardly*. Faith is the root, belief the tree, and opinion the foliage that falls and is renewed with the seasons.

Opinion is, at best, even the opinion of a true man, but the cloak of his belief, which he may indeed cast to his neighbor, but not with the truth inside it. That remains in his own bosom, the oneness between him and his God. St. Paul knows well—who better?—that by no argument, the best that logic itself can afford, can a man be set right with the truth. He knows that the spiritual perception which comes of hungering contact with the living truth—a perception which is in itself a being born again—can alone be the mediator between a man and the truth. He knows that, even if he could pass his opinion over bodily into the understanding of his neighbor, there would be little or nothing gained from it. For the man's spiritual condition would be just what it was before.

God must reveal, or nothing is known. And this, through thousands of difficulties occasioned by the man himself, God is ever and always doing his mighty best to accomplish.

— UNITY AND LOVE IN SPITE OF —
DIFFERING SPIRITUAL DEDICATION

Observe the grandeur of redeeming liberality in the apostle. In his heart of hearts he knows that salvation consists in *nothing* other than being one with Christ. He knows that the *only* true life of every man is hid with Christ in God and to be found by no search anywhere else. He believes that for this cause was he born into the world—that he should give himself, heart and soul, body and spirit, to him who came into the world that he might bear witness to the truth. He believes that for the sake of this, and nothing less—anything more there cannot be—was the world, with its endless glories, created. And even more than all this, he believes that for this did the Lord—in whose cross, type and triumph of his self-abnegation, he glories—come into the world and live and die there.

And yet he says, and says plainly, that a man thinking *differently* from all this, or at least quite unprepared to make this wholehearted profession of faith, is yet his brother in Christ. Even in such a one he believes that the knowledge of Christ, such as it is, will work, the new leaven casting out the old leaven until he too, in the revelation of the Father, shall come to the perfect stature of the fullness of Christ.

In the meantime, Paul the apostle will show due reverence to the halting and dull disciple. He must and will make no demand upon him on the grounds of what he, Paul, believes. The man is where he is, and God is his teacher. To his own Master—that is, Paul's Master, and not Paul—he stands. Paul leaves him to the company of his Master.

"Leaves him?" No, he does not do that. That he will never do, any more than God will leave him. Still and always will Paul do his utmost to hold him and help him.

— PAUL WILL PRESS . . . BUT NOT FOR OPINION —

But how can he help him if he is not to press upon him his own larger and deeper and wiser insights?

The answer is clear. Paul *will* press, but not his opinion, not even the man's own opinion. But he will press the man's own faith upon him.

"O brother, beloved of the Father, walk in the light—in the light, that is, which is yours, not which is mine. Walk in the light that is given to you, not to me. You cannot walk by *my* light, I cannot walk by *yours*. How should anyone walk except by the light which is in him? O brother, what you see, that *do*. And what you do not see, that you shall see. God himself, the Father of lights, will show it to you."

This is the condition of all growth—that what we have attained, we heed the same. Following the oldest manuscripts, this seems to me the apostle's meaning.

— PAUL CLINGS TO UNITY —

Obedience is the one condition of progress, and Paul entreats them to obey. If a man will but work that which is in him, will but make the power of God his own, then it will go well with him forevermore. Like his Master, Paul urges to *action*, to the highest operation, therefore to the highest condition of humanity. As Christ was the Son of his father because he did the will of the Father, so the apostle would have them be the sons of their father by *doing* the will of the Father.

Whereto you have attained, walk by *that*.

But there is more involved in this utterance than the words themselves will expressly carry. Next to his love to the Father and the Elder Brother, the passion of Paul's life—I cannot call it less—is love to all his brothers and sisters. Everything human is dear to him: He can part with none of it. He cannot endure division, separation, the breaking of the body of Christ. The body of his flesh had once been broken that a grander body might be prepared for him. Was it for that spiritual body that would arise later to tear itself asunder?

With the whole energy of his great heart, Paul clung to unity. He could clasp together with might and main the body of his Master—the body that Master loved because it was a spiritual body, with the life of his father in it. And he knew well that only by walking in the truth to which they had attained could they ever draw near to each other. Whereto we have attained, let us walk by that.

My honored friends, if we are not practical, we are nothing. Now, the one main fault in the Christian church is separation, repulsion, recoil between the component particles of the Lord's body. I will not, I do not care to inquire who is more to blame than another in the evil fact. I only care to insist that it is the duty of every individual man and woman to be innocent of the same. One main cause, perhaps I should say *the one* cause of this deathly condition, is that whereto we had, we did *not,* whereto we have attained, we do not *walk* by that.

Ah, friend! Do not now think of your neighbour. Do not applaud my opinion as right from what you have seen around you, but answer it from your *own* being and your *own* behavior. Do you ever feel thus toward your neighbor:

"Yes, of course, every man is my brother. But how can I be a brother to him so long as he thinks me wrong in what I believe, and so long as I think him wrong in his opinions and against the dignity of the truth?"

I return: Has the man no hand that you might grasp, no eyes into which yours might gaze far deeper than your vaunted intellect can follow? Is there not, I ask, anything in him to love? Who said you were to be of one opinion? It is the Lord who asks you to be of one *heart.* Does the Lord love the man? Can the Lord love where there is nothing to love? Are you wiser than he, inasmuch as you perceive impossibility where he has failed to discover it?

Or will you say, "Let the Lord love where he pleases. I will love where I please."

Perhaps you will yield to what I suggest by saying, "Well, I suppose I must, and therefore I will—but with certain reservations, politely quiet in my own heart"?

Or will you speak none of these judgments against your brother but do them all, one after the other, in the secret chambers of your proud spirit? One who delights to condemn is a wounder, a divider of the oneness of Christ. One who prides himself on his loftier vision, and is haughty to his neighbor, is himself a division and has reason to ask: "Am I a particle of Christ's body at all?"

The Master will deal with you on that score. Let it humble you to know that your dearest opinion, the one you worship as if it, and not God, were your Saviour, this very opinion you are doomed to change. For if it works for death within you and not for life, it cannot possibly be right.

— WALKING IN WHAT TRUTH WE KNOW —

Friends, you have done me the honour and kindness to ask me to speak to you. I will speak plainly. I come before you neither hiding anything of my belief, nor foolishly imagining I can transfer my opinions into your hearts. If there is one role I hate, it is that of the proselytizer.

But shall I not come to you as a brother to brethren? Shall I not use the privilege of your invitation and of the place in which I stand—nay, *must* I not myself be obedient to the heavenly vision—in urging you with all the power of my persuasion to set yourself afresh to *walk* according to that which you have attained?

In so doing, whatever yet there is to learn, you shall learn it. Thus doing, and thus only, can you draw nigh to the centre-truth. Thus doing, and thus *only*, shall we draw nigh to each other and become brothers and sisters in Christ, caring for each other's honour and righteousness and true well-being.

It is to them that keep his commandments that he

and his father will come to take up their abode with them.

Whether you or I have the larger share of the truth in that which we hold, of this I am sure, that it is to them that *keep* his commandments that it shall be given to eat of the tree of life.

— I WILL NOT DISPUTE OVER MY BELIEFS —

I believe that Jesus is the eternal Son of the eternal Father. I believe that in him the ideal humanity sat enthroned from all eternity. I believe that as he is the divine man, so is he the human God. I believe that there was no taking of our nature upon himself but the showing of himself as he really was, and that he did this from evermore.

These things, friends, I believe, though never would I be guilty of what in me would be the irreverence of opening my mouth to dispute upon them with another who did not so believe. Not for a moment would I endeavor by argument to convince another of this, my opinion. If it be true, it is God's work to show it, for logic cannot.

But the more, and not the less, do I believe that he, who is no respecter of persons, will, least of all, respect the person of him who thinks to please him by respecting his person and calling him "Lord, Lord" and not doing the things that he tells him. Even if I be right, friend, and you wrong, to you who *do* his commandments more faithfully than I, will the more abundant entrance be administered. God grant that, when you are admitted first, I may not be cast out, but admitted to learn of you that it is truth in the inward parts that he requires. They that have that inward truth, and they alone, shall forever know wisdom.

Bear with me, friends, for I love and honour you. I seek but to stir up your hearts, as I would daily stir up my own, to be true to that which is deepest in us—the voice and the will of the Father of our spirits.

— HOW TO SPREAD THE TRUTH —

Friends, I have not said we are not to speak our opinions. I have only said we are not to make those opinions the point of a fresh start, the foundation of a new building, the groundwork of anything. *Opinions are not to occupy us in our dealings with our brethren.*

Opinion is often the very death of love. Love aright, and you will come to think aright. And those who think aright must think the same.

In the meantime, it matters nothing. The thing that does matter is, that whereto we have attained, by that we should walk. But, while we are not to insist upon our *opinions*, which is the only one way of insisting upon ourselves—however we may cloak the fact from ourselves in the vain imagination of thereby spreading the truth—we *are* bound by the loftiest duty to spread the truth. For that is the saving of men.

Do you ask, "How spread it, if we are not to talk about it?"

Friends, I never said, "Do not talk about the truth." But I do insist upon a better and the only indispensable way of spreading truth—let your light shine. By that loftiest duty we are to spread the truth.

What I said before, and say again, is, "Do not talk about the lantern that holds the lamp, but make haste, uncover the light, and let it shine. Let your light so shine before men that they may see your good works"—I incline to the Vatican reading of *good things*—"and glorify your Father who is in heaven."

It is not, *Let your good works shine*, but *Let your light shine*.

Let it be the genuine love of your hearts, taking form in true deeds, not the doing of good deeds to prove that your opinions are right. If you are thus true, your very talk about the truth will be a good work, a shining of the light that is in you. A true smile is a good work and may do much to reveal the Father who is in heaven. But the smile that is put on for the sake of looking right, or even for the sake of being right, will hardly reveal him because it is not like him.

Men say that you are cold. If you fear it may be so, do not think to make yourselves warm by putting on the cloak of this or that fresh opinion. Draw nearer to the central heat, the living humanity of the Son of Man, that you may have life in yourselves, heat in yourselves, light in yourselves. Understand him, obey him, then your light will shine, and your warmth will warm.

— BY GOODNESS, TRUTH WILL EMERGE —

There is an infection in good just as there is in evil. The better we are, the more will men glorify God. If we trim our lamps so that we have light in our house, that light will shine through our windows and give light to those who are not in the house. But remember, love of the light alone can trim the lamp.

The man who holds his opinion the most honestly ought to see the most plainly that his opinion must change. It is impossible a man should hold anything aright. How shall the created embrace the self-existent Creator? That Creator, and he alone, is the truth.

How, then, shall a man embrace the truth? *To him who will live it*—to him, that is, who walks by that to which he has attained—*the truth will reach down a thousand true hands for his to grasp.* We would not wish to enclose that which we can do more than enclose—live in, namely, as our home, inherit, exult in—the presence of the infinitely higher and better, the heart of the Living One. And, if we know that God himself is our inheritance, why should we tremble even with hatred at the suggestion that we may, that we must, change our opinions?

— OPINIONS MUST CHANGE —

If we held opinions aright, we should know that nothing in them that is good can ever be lost, for that is the true, whatever in them may be the false. It is only as they help us toward God that our opinions are worth a straw. And every necessary change in them must be to more truth, to greater uplifting power.

Lord, change me as thou wilt, only do not send me away. That in my opinions for which I really hold them, if I be a true man, will never pass away. That which my evils and imperfections have, in the process of embodying it, associated with the truth, must, thank God, perish and fall. My opinions, as my life, as my love, I leave in the hands of him from whom all came.

Why, then, is there such dislike to the very idea of change of our ideas, that dread of having to accept the thing offered by those whom we count our opponents, which is such a stumbling block in the way in which we have to walk, such an obstruction to our yet inevitable growth? It may be objected that no man will hold his opinions with the needful earnestness who can entertain the idea of having to change them. But the very objection speaks powerfully against such an overvaluing of opinion. For what is it but to say that, in order to be wise, a man must consent to be a fool.

Whatever must be, a man *must be* able to look in the face. It is because we cleave to our opinions rather than to the living God, because self and pride interest themselves for their own vile sakes with that which belongs only to the truth, that we become such fools of logic and temper that we lie in the prison-houses of our own fancies, ideas, and experiences, shut the doors and windows against the entrance of the free spirit, and will not inherit the love of the Father.

Yet, for the help and comfort of even such a refuser as this, I would say:

Nothing which you reject can be such as it seems to you. For a thing is either true or untrue. If it be untrue, it looks so far like itself that you reject it, and with it we have nothing more to do. But if it is true, the very fact that you reject it shows that to you it has not appeared true—has not appeared itself.

The truth can never be even beheld but by the man who accepts it. The thing, therefore, which you reject, is not that which it seems to you, but a thing good, and altogether beautiful, altogether fit for your gladsome embrace—a thing from which you would not turn away, did you see it as it is, but rush to it, as Dante says, "like the wild beast to his den"—so eager for the refuge of home. No honest man holds a truth for the sake of that because of which another honest man rejects it. How it may be with the dishonest man, I have no confidence in my judgment and hope I am not bound to understand.

— LIGHT, NOT PERSUASION —

Let us then, my friends, beware lest our opinions come between us and our God, between us and our neighbor, between us and our better selves. Let us be jealous that the human shall not obscure the divine. For we are not *merely* human—we also are divine. And there is no such obliterator of the divine as the human that acts undivinely. The one security against our opinions is to walk according to the truth which they contain.

And if men seem to us unreasonable, opposers of that which to us is plainly true, let us remember that we are not here to convince men, but to let our light shine.

Knowledge is not necessarily light. And it is light, not knowledge, that we have to spread. The best thing we can do—infinitely the best, indeed the only thing—that men may receive the truth, *is to be ourselves true*. Beyond all doing of good is the *being* good, for he that is good not only does good things, but all that he does is good.

Above all, let us be humble before the God of truth, faithfully desiring of him that truth in the inward parts which alone can enable us to walk according to that which we have attained.

May the God of peace give you his peace. May the love of Christ constrain you. May the gift of the Holy Spirit be yours. *And may we all, beholding the glory of the Lord, be changed into the same likeness.*

Insights Into

Opinion and Truth

MICHAEL PHILLIPS

— THE CLOAK SURROUNDING TRUTH —

The selection you have just read was originally entitled merely "A Sermon." It was read by George MacDonald in the Unitarian chapel on Essex Street, London, in 1879, and was published in the book called *A Dish of Orts*. I have given it the title "Opinion and Truth" in order to help clarify its foundational thesis. In a sense there is not a great deal more to be said than this: *Opinion is not truth.*

So much, however, of what throughout history has comprised, and continues to comprise, the energy of the Christian church and its belief systems is built upon the former rather than the latter. Therefore, it is worth a few moments of our reflection to consider the difference between the two.

MacDonald distinguishes between opinion and truth by indicating that "opinion is merely the intellectual body of truth"—the outer shell by which we put into words deeper truths too large to be framed by words at all. Opinion, therefore, *may* point truly toward, and *may* be an accurate representation of, truth, but only when "the needle of a man's moral compass" is capable of pointing truly.

Nevertheless, it is clear that in many cases something is "lost in translation" in moving from the inner to the outer. Especially is this true whenever one individual tries to communicate to another what that second individual may mistake, misunderstand, or receive through ears biased because of his *own* opinions to mishear *another's*. Thus a right reception of truth almost never results when one individual attempts to force his or her opinions on another.

I am reminded of MacDonald's wonderful aside in *Thomas Wingfold, Curate*:

> Generally, in any talk worth calling conversation, every man has some point to maintain, and his object is to justify his own thesis and disprove his neighbour's. I will allow that he may primarily have adopted his thesis because of some sign of truth in it, but his mode of supporting it is generally such as to block up every cranny in his soul at which more truth might enter.

The value and legitimacy of opinions has more to do with the person himself or herself, and his or her truthfulness *as an individual*, than it does with the actual opinions themselves. The opinions of a true man will weigh more than the opinions of a fool, because they will be more likely to point accurately toward truth.

The worst result . . . [is] the false and arrogant notion that it is one's duty to force one's opinion upon the acceptance of others.

Such men themselves hold with poor grasp the truth underlying the forms of their opinions. They are, in their self-sufficiency, so ambitious of propagating the *forms* that they actually make of themselves the worst enemies of the *truth* of which they fancy themselves the champions.

How truly, in the case of all genuine teachers of men, shall a man's foes be they of his own household! . . . So many of them have received but the *forms* and know nothing of the *truth* which gave him those forms! . . .

Opinions so held belong to the theology of hell. They are not necessarily altogether false in form, but they are utterly false in heart and spirit.

The opinion that is hurtful is not that which is formed in the depths and from the honest necessities of a man's own nature, but that which he has taken up secondhand, the study of which has pleased his intellect. . . . Some of them have puffed him up with a sense of superiority as false as it is foolish, placing in his hand a club with which to intellectually subjugate his neighbour to his spiritual dictation.

Even the true man, who aims at the perpetuation of his opinion, is obstructing rather than aiding the course of that truth for the love of which he holds his opinion in the first place. *For truth is a*

living thing, opinion is a dead thing, and transmit-
ted opinion a deadening thing.

MacDonald goes on, using Paul as his example, to illuminate the role of opinion in belief and faith, in which he calls opinion "the cloak of belief."

This is Paul's faith, not his opinion. Faith is that by which a man lives *inwardly* and orders his way *out-wardly*. Faith is the root, belief the tree, and opin-ion the foliage that falls and is renewed with the seasons.

Opinion is, at best, even the opinion of a true man, but the cloak of his belief, which he may indeed cast to his neighbour, but not with the truth inside it. That remains in his own bosom, the one-ness between him and his God. St. Paul knows well—who better?—that by no argument . . . can a man be set right with the truth. He knows that the spiritual perception which comes of hungering con-tact with the living truth . . . can alone be the mediator between a man and the truth. He knows that, even if he could pass his opinion over bodily into the understanding of his neighbour, there would be little or nothing gained from it. For the man's spiritual condition would be just what it was before.

God must reveal, or nothing is known. And this, through thousands of difficulties occasioned by the man himself, God is ever and always doing his mighty best to accomplish.

Because of these distinctions, Paul never presses

opinion, only faith. Is this why MacDonald always spoke so persistently against dispute over doctrinal matters? Unity, not divergent doctrinal opinions, and certainly not attempted *persuasion* about those opinions, was for him the high objective toward which interrelationship between Christians all should aim.

> With the whole energy of his great heart, Paul clung to unity. . . . And he knew well that only by walking in the truth to which they had attained could they ever draw near to each other. Whereto we have attained, let us walk by that.

— AGAINST PERSUASION: A PERSONAL GLIMPSE —

It is not often we get such a personal glimpse into MacDonald himself as here reveals itself through the medium of what was originally a "spoken" sermon. It stirs my pulse a little to imagine what it might have been like to sit in that congregation listening to these words in MacDonald's polished Scots inflection.

> Friends, you have done me the honour and kindness to ask me to speak to you. I will speak plainly. I come before you neither hiding anything of my belief nor foolishly imagining I can transfer my opinions into your hearts. If there is one role I hate, it is that of the proselytizer.
>
> But shall I not come to you as a brother to brethren? Shall I not use the privilege of your invitation . . . in urging you with all the power of my persuasion to set yourself afresh to *walk* according to that which you have attained?

In so doing, whatever yet there is to learn, you
shall learn it. Thus doing, and thus only, can you
draw nigh to the centre-truth. Thus doing, and thus
only, shall we draw nigh to each other and become
brothers and sisters in Christ. . . . It is to them that
keep his commandments that he and his father will
come to take up their abode with them.

Whether you or I have the larger share of the
truth in that which we hold, of this I am sure, that
it is to them that *keep* his commandments that it
shall be given to eat of the tree of life.

Though brief, I find MacDonald's comments in the
selection on the Father-Son relationship so intriguing for
what they reveal between the lines that I consider the
matter worthy of an explanatory tangent.

Late-nineteenth-century Great Britain was a positive
intellectual greenhouse for radical new ideas in many
fields, from politics to science to theology. Liberal trends
were pushing beyond boundaries which would have been
inconceivable a hundred years before. Societal concerns
gave rise to socialism. On its heels, communism was
born in England during the century's final two decades.
Scientific advances changed the way people viewed the
natural world. Darwin had already proposed an evolu-
tionary foundation for the animal kingdom. Within the
first decade of the twentieth century Einstein would
propose his special theory of relativity.

This ideological surge brought with it rapid and enormous change. The British monarchy was quickly losing
power and influence. The industrial revolution was causing political and cultural upheaval. Electricity changed
living conditions, the telephone changed communica-

tions, and motorized engines changed transportation. Cities were doubling in size every few years as society became increasingly urban. Parliament, once a bastion of conservatism and aristocracy, was undergoing the infancy of the Labour Party. The middle class was rising in influence. All men, not just nobles, could vote, and that right would soon come to women as well.

In such an historic milieu, a climate of vigorous rationalism characterized the latter years of the Victorian era, causing a reevaluation of traditional norms in every discipline and walk of life. This questioning and debating outlook was evident everywhere. Whereas the debate between God and science, evolution and creation, took place mostly between the conservative church and the scientific community, other equally heated controversies existed *within* the church. No more divisive point of contention existed among Christians than the theological uproar over "universalism," or, more properly, *universal reconciliation*. This dispute furiously raged in all denominations and seminaries, split churches, and resulted in thousands of books, pamphlets, and parlor debates throughout England and Scotland. As today, belief in universal reconciliation was considered heresy in some circles, enlightened thinking in others.

There were many areas of dispute and doctrinal division besides evolution and universalism. Notable examples include the Trinity and the Atonement, over which the discourse centered upon who Jesus was and what his work on the cross actually accomplished.

As a bold thinker unafraid of spiritual inquiry, George MacDonald was intrigued by all such debate. And because he believed so strongly in an expansive, embracing Father-God of infinite love who would shun no line of thought, for most of his public career he was considered unorthodox by the Calvinist wing of the Protestant church, out of which he himself had come. Because he could appear so theologically liberal one minute and so downright traditional the next, people never quite knew what to do with him: He defied pigeonhole analysis.

Both during his lifetime and today, then, MacDonald was and is a controversial figure in the history of the church and its theology. Even as a youth his uncommon and expansive views were apparently of concern to the family of the young woman who would become his wife (for over fifty years). The future Louisa MacDonald would not accept his proposal of marriage until he had addressed himself satisfactorily on the Atonement. A few years later some in the congregation of the only church whose pulpit MacDonald occupied as pastor were concerned that he had been too influenced by German mysticism, and they were later scandalized at his conviction that animals would be present in heaven.

But George MacDonald did not care about being considered "orthodox" any more than he cared about provoking dispute by being controversial. He sought only truth—however it came. Once convinced of it, he would proclaim it fearlessly.

In this light, I always find fascinating his comment in "The Creation in Christ," also regarding the Trinity: "I write with no desire to provoke controversy, which I loathe, but with some hope of presenting to the minds of those capable of seeing it the glory of the truth of the Father and the Son. . . . I am as indifferent to a reputation for orthodoxy as I despise the championship of novelty."

The Unitarian Church in England had grown rapidly during the nineteenth century. By the 1870s, when MacDonald delivered this sermon, Unitarianism was a major force in the climate of theological debate because of its rigid rejection of the Trinity. While on this particular doctrine MacDonald's ideas (though imaginative and far-reaching) were mostly traditional and Trinitarian, curiously, he was highly sought after by the Unitarians as a guest minister. His son Ronald says that his father accepted invitations to Unitarian pulpits only after clarifying that he must be free to speak about the Trinity.

Ronald wrote:

> After his abandonment of the predicant profession, he never took remuneration for a spoken sermon; and never, I am sure, refused his preaching, from whatever Christian denomination the invitation might come. I remember very well his saying that the Unitarians were among the most instant to get him to preach; and that he always stipulated for liberty to maintain the doctrine of the Trinity; by which orthodoxy I do not think he ever gained a Sunday's rest. (Ronald MacDonald, *From a Northern Window: A Personal Remembrance of George MacDonald*, first published by James Nisbet & Co., London, 1911. Available from Sunrise Books, Box 7003, Eureka, CA 95502)

Ronald's comments wonderfully illuminate his father's words in the following passage. We can almost hear MacDonald's voice, tenderly and compassionately yet urgently imploring the Unitarian congregation, emphasizing his "opinion" concerning the relationship between Father and Son in the Godhead, not to persuade, as he says, but to rouse obedience.

> I believe that Jesus is the eternal Son of the eternal Father. I believe that in him the ideal humanity sat enthroned from all eternity. I believe that as he is the divine man, so is he the human God. I believe that there was no taking of our nature upon himself, but the showing of himself as he really was, and that he did this from evermore.
>
> These things, friends, I believe, though never would I be guilty of what in me would be the irreverence of opening my mouth to dispute upon them. . . . Not for a moment would I endeavor by argument to convince another of this, my opinion. If it be true, it is God's work to show it, for logic cannot. . . .
>
> Bear with me, friends, for I love and honour you. I seek but to stir up your hearts, as I would daily stir up my own, to be true to that which is deepest in us—the voice and the will of the Father of our spirits.

— WE MUST WALK IN TRUTH, NOT OPINION —

MacDonald concludes, where we knew he must, by saying yet again that opinion matters nothing, obedience everything.

> Friends, I have not said we are not to speak our opinions. I have only said we are not to make those

opinions . . . the foundation . . . of anything. *Opinions are not to occupy us in our dealings with our brethren.*

Opinion is often the very death of love. Love aright, and you will come to think aright. And those who think aright must think the same.

In the meantime, it matters nothing. The thing that does matter is that whereto we have attained by that we should walk. . . .

How, then, shall a man embrace the truth? *To him who will live it*—to him, that is, who walks by that to which he has attained—*the truth will reach down a thousand true hands for his to grasp. . . .*

Let us then, my friends, beware lest our opinions come between us and our God, between us and our neighbor, between us and our better selves. Let us be jealous that the human shall not obscure the divine. For we are not *merely* human—we also are divine. . . .

The one security against our opinions is to walk according to the truth which they contain.

*But we all, with open face beholding
as in a glass the glory of the Lord,
are changed into the same image
from glory to glory, even as
by the spirit of the Lord.*

—2 CORINTHIANS 3:18

The Mirrors
of the Lord

GEORGE MACDONALD

We may see from this passage how the apostle Paul received the Lord, and how he understands Christ's life to be the light of men, and so their life also.

— MYSTERY AND PRACTICALITY —

Of all the writers I know, Paul seems to me the most plainly, the most determinedly *practical* in his writing. What has been called his mysticism is sometimes but the exercise of an extraordinary power of seeing, as by spiritual refraction, truths that had not, perhaps have not yet, risen above the human horizon. At other times his spiritual vision is the result of a wide-eyed habit of noting the analogies and correspondences between the concentric regions of creation. It is the working of a poetic imagination divinely alive, whose part is to foresee and welcome approaching truth. He discovers the same principle in things that look unalike, embodies things discovered in forms and symbols previously unused, and so presents to other minds the deeper truths to which forms and symbols owe their being.

I find in Paul's writing the same artistic fault, with the same resulting difficulty, that I find in Shakespeare's—a fault that, in each case, springs from the admirable fact that the man is much more than the artist. It is the fault of trying to say too much at once, of pouring out stintless the plethora of a soul, swelling with life and its thought, through the too-narrow neck of human utterance.

Thence it comes that we are at times bewildered between two or more meanings, equally good in themselves but perplexing as to the right deduction regarding the line of the thinker's reasoning.

Such uncertainties, however, always lie in the intellectual region, never in the practical. What Paul cares about is plain enough to the true heart, however far from plain they may be to the man whose desire to understand goes ahead of his obedience. Such men start with the notion that Paul's design was to teach a system of theology. They think that his desire was to explain, instead of help to see God, a God that can be revealed only to childlike insight, never to keenest intellect.

The energy of the apostle, like that of his master, went forth to rouse men to seek the kingdom of God over them and his righteousness in them. His desire was to dismiss the lust of possession and passing pleasure in the hearts of his hearers, that they might look upon the glory of the God and Father and turn to him from all that he hates, recognizing the brotherhood of men and the hideousness of what is unfair, unloving, and self-exalting.

Paul's design was not to teach any plan of salvation other than obedience to the Lord of life. He knew nothing of the so-called Christian systems that change the glory of the perfect God into the likeness of the low intellects and dull consciences of men—a worse corruption than the representing of him in human shape. What kind of soul is it that would not choose the Apollo of light, a mighty Titan, to the notion of the dull, self-cherishing monarch, the law-dispensing magistrate, or the cruel martinet, generated in the pagan arrogance of Rome and accepted by the world in the church as the portrait of its God!

Jesus Christ is the *only* likeness of the living Father.

Let us see then what Paul teaches us in this passage about the life which is the light of men. It is his form of bringing to bear upon men the truth announced by John.

— A VEIL OVER THE HEART —

When Moses came out from speaking with God, his face was radiant. Its shining was a wonder to the people and a power upon them. But the radiance began at once to diminish and die away, as was natural, for it was not indigenous in Moses. Therefore Moses put a veil upon his face that they might not see it fade. As to whether this was right or wise, opinion may differ. It is not my business to discuss the question. When he went again into the tabernacle, he took off his veil, talked with God with open face, and again put on the veil when he came out. Paul says that the veil which obscured the face of Moses lies now upon the hearts of the Jews, so that they cannot understand him, but that when they turn to the Lord, go into the tabernacle with Moses, the veil shall be taken away, and they shall see God. Then will they understand that the glory is indeed faded upon the face of Moses, but because of the glory that excels, the glory of Jesus that overshines it.

Here, after all, I can hardly help asking—would not Moses have done better to let them see that the glory of their leader was altogether dependent on the glory within the veil, where they were not worthy to enter?

Did that veil hide Moses' face only? Did he not, however unintentionally, lay it also on their hearts? Did the veil not cling there, and help to hide God from them, so that they could not perceive that one greater than Moses was come and stormed at the idea that the glory of their prophet must yield? Might not the absence of that veil from his face have left them a little more able to realize that his glory was a glory that must pass, a glory whose glory prepared the way for a glory that must extinguish it?

Moses removed the veil forever from his face, but they clutched it to their hearts, and it blinded them. What an admirable symbol of the willful blindness of the old Mosaist or modern Wesleyan, admitting no light that his Moses or his Wesley did not see, and thus losing what of the light he saw and reflected.

Paul says that the sight of the Lord will take that veil from their hearts. His light will burn it away. His presence gives liberty. Where he is, there is no more heaviness, no more bondage, no more wilderness or Mount Sinai. The Son makes free with sonship.

And now comes the passage whose import I desire to make more clear:

"But we all," having this presence and this liberty, "with open face beholding as in a glass the glory of the Lord, are changed into the same image," that of the Lord, "from glory to glory, even as of the Lord, the spirit."

"We need no Moses, no earthly mediator," I imagine Paul saying, "to come between us and the light, and bring out for us a *little* of the glory. We go ourselves into the presence of the Son revealing the Father—into the presence of the Light of men. Our mediator is the Lord himself, the spirit of light. He is a mediator not sent by us to God to bring back his will, but who is come from God to bring us *himself*. We enter, like Moses, into the presence of the visible, radiant God—only how much more visible and more radiant!

"As Moses stood with uncovered face receiving the glory of God full upon it, so with open uncovered face, full in the light of the glory of God, in the place of his presence, we also stand—you and I, Corinthians. It is no reflected light we see, but the glory of God shining in, shining out of, shining *in and from* the face of Christ, the glory of the Father, one with the Son. Israel saw but the fading reflection of the glory of God on the face of Moses. We see the glory itself in the face of Jesus."

— TO MIRROR —

In what follows, though, it seems to me that the Revised Version misses the meaning almost as much as the Authorized, when, instead of "beholding as in a glass," it gives "reflecting as a mirror." The former is wrong. The latter is far from right. The idea, with the image, is that of a poet, not a man of science. The poet deals with the outer show of things, which outer show is infinitely deeper in its relation to truth, as well as more practically useful than the analysis of the man of science. Paul never thought of the mirror as reflecting, as throwing back the rays of light from its surface. He thought of it as *receiving*, taking into itself, the things presented to it—in this case, as filling its bosom with the glory it looks upon.

When I see the face of my friend in a mirror, the mirror seems to hold it in itself, to surround the visage with its liquid embrace. The countenance is *there*—down there in the depth of the mirror. True, it shines radiant out of it, but it is not the shining out of it that Paul has in his thought. It is the fact—the *visual* fact, which, according to Wordsworth, the poet always seizes—of the mirror holding in it the face.

This is the way poet or prophet—Paul was both—would think of the thing, especially in the age of the apostle. I shall be able to make this meaning appear even more probable by directing your notice to the following passage from Dante—whose time, though so much farther from that of the apostle than our time from Dante's, was in many respects much more like Paul's than ours.

The passage is this:

> *E quei: "S' io fossi d' impiombato vetro,*
> *L' immagine di fuor tua non trarrei*
> *Piu tosto a me, che quella dentro impetro."*
> (*Inferno*, C. xxiii, 25–27)

Here Virgil, with reference to the power he had of reading the thoughts of his companion, says to Dante: "If I were of leaded glass" (meaning, *If I were glass covered at the back with lead, so that I was a mirror*), "I should not draw thy outward image to me more readily than I gain thy inner one" (meaning, *I shall now see your appearance more than now I know your thoughts*).

It seems, then, to me, that the true simple word to represent the Greek, and the most literal as well by which to translate it, is the verb *mirror*—when the sentence, so far, would run thus: "But we all, with unveiled face, mirroring the glory of the Lord. . . ."

— PAUL'S MEANING —

I must now go on to unfold the idea at work in the heart of the apostle. For the mere correctness of a translation is nothing in itself, except it bring us something deeper, or at least some fresher insight. I will not concern myself with him who cares for the words apart from what the writer meant them to convey. To such I say: You must cease to "pass for a man" and begin to be a man indeed, on the way to being a live soul, before I can desire relation with you.

The prophet-apostle seems to me, then, to say, "We all, with clear vision of the Lord, mirroring in our hearts his glory, even as a mirror would take into itself his face, are thereby changed into his likeness, his glory working our glory, by the present power, in our inmost being, of the Lord, the spirit."

Thus our mirroring of Christ is one with the presence of his spirit in us. The idea, you see, is not the reflection, the *radiating* of the light of Christ to others, though that is an appropriate enough image in its own right, but rather the taking *into,* and having *in* us, him working *to the changing of us.*

It is no great discovery that the thing signified transcends the sign, outreaches the figure. The thing figured always belongs to a higher stratum, to which the simile serves but as a ladder. When the climber has reached it, "he then unto the ladder turns his back." It is but according to the law of imagery and symbols that the thing symbolized by the mirror should have properties far *beyond* those of leaded glass or polished metal. It is a live soul understanding that which it takes into its deeps—holding it, and conscious of what it holds. It mirrors by its will to hold in its mirror. Unlike its symbol, it can hold not merely the outward visual resemblance, but the inward likeness of the person revealed by it. It is open to the influences of that which it embraces, and is capable of active cooperation with them. The mirror and the thing mirrored are of one origin and nature and in closest relation to each other.

Paul's idea is that when we take into our understanding, our heart, our conscience, our being, the glory of God, namely, Jesus Christ as he shows himself to our eyes and hearts and consciences, he works upon us and will keep working till we are changed to the very likeness we have thus mirrored in us. For *with his likeness he comes himself, and dwells in us.* He will work until the same likeness is wrought out and perfected in us, the image, namely, of the humanity of God, in which image we were made at first, but which could never be developed in us except by the indwelling of the perfect likeness. By the power of Christ thus received and at home in us, we are changed—the glory in him becoming glory in us, his glory changing us to glory.

— HE COMES *IN* —

We must beware of receiving this or any symbol *after the flesh*, beware of interpreting it in any fashion that partakes of the character of the mere physical, psychical, or spirituo-mechanical. Symbols deal with things far beyond the deepest region from which symbols can be drawn. Who shall comprehend, with mere symbols, the indwelling of Jesus in the soul of man!

But let us note this, that the dwelling of Jesus in us is the power of the spirit of God upon us. For "the Lord is that spirit." And with that Lord dwelling in us, we are changed "even as from the Lord the spirit." When we think Christ, Christ *comes*. When we receive his image into our spiritual mirror, *he enters with it*. Our thought is not cut off from his. Our *open receiving thought* is his door to come in. When our hearts turn to him, that heart-turning opens the door to him by holding up our mirror to him. And he comes in, not only by our thought, not only in our idea, but he comes *himself*, and of his own will. He comes in as we could not take him, but as he can come and as we can receive him. We are enabled to receive by his very coming the one welcome guest of the whole universe.

Thus the Lord, the spirit, becomes the soul of our souls, becomes *spiritually* what he always was *creatively*. And as our spirit informs and gives shape to our bodies, in like manner his soul informs and gives shape to our *souls*.

In this there is nothing unnatural, nothing at conflict with our being. It is but that the deeper soul that willed and wills our souls, rises up, the infinite Life, into the self we call *I* and *me*, but which lives immediately from him and is his very own property and nature—unspeakably more his than ours. This deeper creative soul, working on and with his creation upon higher levels, makes the *I* and *me* more and more his, and himself more and more ours. At length, the glory of our existence will flash upon us as we face full to the sun that enlightens what it sent forth. Then will we know ourselves alive with an infinite life, even the life of the Father. Then we will know that our existence is not the moonlight of a mere consciousness of being. Rather it is the sun-glory of a life justified by having become one with its origin, thinking and feeling with the primal Sun of life, from whom it was dropped away that it might know and bethink itself, and return to circle for ever in exultant harmony around him.

— LIFE BECOMES LIFE WITHIN US —

Then indeed we *are*. Then indeed we have life. The life of Jesus has, through light, become life in us. The glory of God in the face of Jesus, mirrored in our hearts, has made us alive. We are one with God for ever and ever.

What less than such a splendour of hope would be worthy of the revelation of Jesus? Filled with the soul of their Father, men shall inherit the glory of their Father. Filled with themselves, they cast him out and rot.

The company of the Lord, soul to soul, is that which saves with life—his life of God-devotion—the souls of his brethren. No other saving can save them. They must receive the Son, and through the Son the Father.

What it cost the Son to get so near to us that we could say *Come in,* is the story of his life. He stands at the door and knocks, and when we open to him he comes in, and dwells with us, and we are transformed to the same image of truth and purity and heavenly childhood.

Where power dwells, there is no force. Where the spirit-Lord is, there is liberty. The Lord Jesus, by free, potent communion with their inmost being, will change his obedient brethren till in every thought and impulse they are good like him, unselfish, neighbourly, brotherly like him, loving the Father perfectly like him, ready to die for the truth like him, caring like him for nothing in the universe but the will of God, which is love, harmony, liberty, beauty, and joy.

I do not know if we may call this having life in ourselves. But it is the waking up, the perfecting in us of the divine life inherited from our Father in heaven, who made us in his own image, whose nature remains in us and makes it the deepest reproach to a man that he has neither heard his voice at any time nor seen his shape.

He who would thus live must, as a mirror draws into its bosom an outward glory, receive into his heart of hearts the inward glory of *Jesus Christ, the Son and the God of the Living.*

Insights Into

The Mirrors
of the Lord

MICHAEL PHILLIPS

It is remarkable how often words from George Mac-
Donald's pen, as we read them now from our perspective a hundred or more years removed, seem propheti-
cally pointed in directions he surely never intended.
Such I find his introductory passage here about Paul and
his writings. For as I read them, the words illuminate
with remarkable precision the indescribable impact
upon Christian thought, not merely of the apostle Paul
but also of George MacDonald. MacDonald frequently
penned unwitting self-portraits (numerous examples
exist in his writings if one knows how to see them), and
surely this is one of the most telling. I would say, and
many others would certainly affirm, *Of all writers I
know, George MacDonald seems the most plainly, the*

most determinedly practical in his writing. What has been called his mysticism is sometimes but the exercise of an extraordinary power of seeing, as by spiritual refraction, truths that had not, perhaps yet have not, risen above the human horizon. At other times, his spiritual vision is the result of a wide-eyed habit of noting the analogies and correspondences between the concentric regions of creation. It is the working of a poetic imagination divinely alive, whose part is to foresee and welcome approaching truth.

It is for exactly the reason that MacDonald here expresses that I have said—perhaps a little too boldly for the palates of some—that I consider his perspective regarding God's character and work on a level with Paul's at certain points in revealing truths that must be seen if we are to understand God aright. MacDonald's was, and is, a prophetic voice because of his "spiritual vision," his "poetic imagination divinely alive," and his "extraordinary power of seeing . . . truths that had not, perhaps yet have not, risen above the human horizon."

One primary reason men have so misunderstood God's character through the years, and why that character remains obscure to so many who call themselves his followers, is that men have constructed "systematic theologies" of belief rather than teaching Christians how to *live*.

This was never his intent in his own writing, and, according to MacDonald, such systematizing was also far from Paul's practical intent. Yet men have built huge theological edifices out of Paul's words that, because practicality and obedience have not been their foundation stones, rise into doctrinal buildings Paul would not even recognize. "Such men," says MacDonald, "start with the notion that Paul's design was to teach a system of theology. They think that his desire was to explain instead of help to see God, a God that can be revealed only to childlike insight, never to keenest intellect."

He continues:

> Paul's design was not to teach any plan of salvation other than obedience to the Lord of life. He knew nothing of the so-called Christian systems that change the glory of the perfect God into the likeness of the low intellects and dull consciences of men—a worse corruption than the representing of him in human shape. What kind of soul is it that would not choose the Apollo of light, a mighty Titan, to the notion of the dull, self-cherishing monarch, the law-dispensing magistrate, or the cruel martinet, generated in the pagan arrogance of Rome and accepted by the world in the church as the portrait of its God!
>
> Jesus Christ is the *only* likeness of the living Father.

As he goes on to take up the subject for which he entitled his sermon "The Mirrors of the Lord" (*Unspoken Sermons, Third Series*), MacDonald returns yet again to oft-repeated themes. God's intent is that we ourselves reflect, not a mere portion or obscure image of his nature and character and glory, but that we rise into the sonship that will actually *be* that nature—not merely reflecting it back, but, having received it *into* ourselves, shining *out* with that nature from within our very beings because we have been fundamentally changed into that nature.

The prophet-apostle seems to me, then, to say, "We all, with clear vision of the Lord, mirroring in our hearts his glory, even as a mirror would take into itself his face, are thereby changed into his likeness . . . by the present power, in our inmost being, of the Lord, the spirit."

Our mirroring of Christ, then . . . is not the reflection, the *radiating* of the light of Christ to others, though that is an appropriate enough image in its own right, but rather the taking *into*, and having *in* us, him working *to the changing of us*.

As sons and daughters, we are being made *like Christ*, transformed into his image, and thus mirroring his image outwardly.

Paul's idea is that when we take into our understanding, our heart, our conscience, our being, the glory of God, namely, Jesus Christ as he shows himself to our eyes and hearts and consciences, he works upon us and will keep working till we are changed to the very likeness we have thus mirrored in us. For *with his likeness he comes himself, and dwells in us*. He will work until the same likeness is wrought out and perfected in us, the image, namely, of the humanity of God, in which image we were made at first. . . . By the power of Christ thus received and at home in us, we are changed— the glory in him becoming glory in us, his glory changing us to glory.

This transformation process occurs by the indwelling within us of the Spirit of Christ.

When we receive his image into our spiritual mirror, *he enters with it.* . . . Our *open receiving thought* is his door to come in. When our hearts turn to him, that heart-turning opens the door to him by holding up our mirror to him. And he comes in, not only by our thought, not only in our idea, but he comes *himself,* and of his own will. He comes in as we could not take him, but as he can come and as we can receive him. We are enabled to receive by his very coming the one welcome guest of the whole universe. . . . And as our spirit informs and gives shape to our bodies, in like manner his soul informs and gives shape to our *souls.*

Only so can we, and will we, truly enter into and partake of life. It is what we were created for. All of life urges us to extend this divine invitation. "Then indeed," says MacDonald, "we *are.*"

The life of Jesus has, through light, become life in us. The glory of God in the face of Jesus, mirrored in our hearts, has made us alive. We are one with God for ever and ever. . . .

What it cost the Son to get so near to us that we could say *Come in,* is the story of his life. He stands at the door and knocks, and when we open to him he comes in, and dwells with us, and we are transformed to the same image of truth and purity and heavenly childhood. . . .

I do not know if we may call this having life in ourselves. But it is the waking up, the perfecting in us of the divine life inherited from our Father in heaven, who made us in his own image, whose nature remains in us.

*He is not a God of the dead, but of the
living: for all live unto him.*

—LUKE 20:38

The God
of the Living

GEORGE MACDONALD

— WHY DID THE SADDUCEES KEEP SILENT? —

It is a recurring cause of perplexity in our Lord's teaching that he is too simple for us. While we are questioning about the design of Solomon's carving upon some gold-plated door of the temple, he is speaking about the foundation of Mount Zion—indeed of the earth itself upon which the temple stands.

If the reader of the gospel supposes that our Lord was using a merely verbal argument with the Sadducees in the above passage from Luke 20—namely, "I *am* the God of Abraham, Isaac, and Jacob; therefore they *are*"—he will be astonished that no Sadducee was found with courage enough to reply.

They might well have refuted him by saying, "All that God meant in Exodus 3 was to introduce himself to Moses as the same God who had aided and protected his fathers while they were alive, saying, I am he that was the God of thy fathers. They found me faithful. Thou, therefore, listen to me, and thou too shalt find me faithful *unto* the death."

But no such reply suggested itself even to the Sadducees of that day. For their Eastern nature could see argument beyond logic. Shall God call himself the God of the dead—of those who were once alive but whom he either could not or would not keep alive?

Is that the Godhead? Is that God's relation to those who worship him? Is he the changeless God of an ever-born and ever-perishing torrent of life, each atom of which cries with burning heart, *My God!* and then passes into the godless cold?

Would God say: "Trust in me, for I took care of your fathers once upon a time, though they are gone now. Worship and obey me, for I will be good to you for threescore years and ten, or thereabouts. After that, when you no longer exist and the world goes on just the same without you, I will still call myself your God."

God changes not. Once God he is always God. If he has once said to a man, "I am thy God," and that man has died the death of the Sadducees' creed, then we have a right to say that God is the God of the dead.

"And what would be wrong with saying that he is the God of the dead, if during the time allotted to them here, he was a faithful God to the living?"

What God-like relationship can the ever-living, life-giving, changeless God have with creatures who partake not of his manner of life, who have death at the very core of their being and are not worth their Maker's keeping alive?

— THEY MUST BE ALIVE —

To let his creatures die would be to repudiate his very Godhood, to cease to be the very being which he had made himself. If they are not worth keeping alive, then his creating is a poor thing and he is not so great, nor so divine, as even the poor thoughts of his dying creatures have been able to imagine him.

But our Lord says, "All live unto him." With Him death is not.

Thy life sees our life, O Lord. All of whom all can be said are present to thee. Thou thinkest about us eternally more than we think about thee. The little life that burns within the body of this death glows unquenchable in thy true-seeing eyes. If thou didst forget us for a moment then indeed death would be our fate. But unto thee we live. The beloved pass from our sight, but they pass not from thine. What we call death is but a form in the eyes of men. It looks like something final, an awful cessation, an utter change. It seems not probable that there is anything beyond. But if God could see us before we were born and make us to conform to his ideal, that we shall have passed from the eyes of our friends can be no argument that he can see us no longer.

"All live unto Him."

Let the change be ever so great, ever so imposing, let the unseen life be ever so vague to our conception, it is not against reason to hope that God could see Abraham, after his Isaac had stopped seeing him, and saw Isaac after Jacob stopped seeing him, and saw Jacob after some of the Sadducees had begun to doubt whether there had ever been a Jacob at all.

He remembers them. That is, he carries them in his mind. And he that God is thinking about must *live*. He calls himself *their* God. The Living One cannot name himself after the dead. The very Godhead lies in the giving of life. Therefore, they must be alive.

If he speaks of them, remembers his own loving thoughts of them, would he not have kept them alive if he could? And if he could not, how could he create them? Can it be an easier thing to *call into life* than to *keep alive*?

"But if they live to God, they are aware of God. And if they are aware of God, they are surely conscious of their own being: Whence comes then the necessity of a resurrection?"

For their relation to others of God's children in mutual revelation, and for fresh revelation of God to all.

But let us inquire what is meant by the resurrection of the body. "With what body do they come into the resurrection?"

— THE RESURRECTION OF THE BODY —

Surely we are not required to believe that our same bodies are raised again. That is against science, common sense, and Scripture. St. Paul represents the matter quite otherwise. One feels ashamed of arguing such a minor point. Who could wish his material body—which has indeed died over and over again since he was born, never remaining for one hour composed of the same matter, its endless activity depending upon its endless change—to be fixed as his changeless possession, especially such as that body may be at the moment of death? Who would want such a body secured to him in worthless identity for the ages to come?

A man's material body will be to his consciousness at death no more than the old garment he throws aside at night, intending to put on a new and a better one in the morning. To desire to keep the old body seems to me to argue a degree of sensual materialism excusable only in those pagans who in their heavenly ideal could hope to possess only such a thin, fleeting, dreamy, and altogether funebrial existence that they might well long for the thicker, more tangible bodily being in which they had experienced the pleasures of a tumultuous life on the upper world. As well might a Christian desire that the hair which has been shorn from him through all his past life should be restored to his risen and glorified head.

Yet not the less is the doctrine of the resurrection gladdening as the sound of the silver trumpet of its visions, needful as the very breath of life to our longing souls. Let us try to discover what it means, and we shall see that it is thus precious.

Let us first ask what is the use of this body of ours. Is it not the means of revelation to us, the *camera* in which God's eternal shows are set forth to our senses? It is by the body that we come into contact with Nature, with our fellow-men, with all their revelations of God to us. It is through the body that we receive all the lessons of passion, suffering, love, beauty, and science. It is through the body that we are both trained outward from ourselves and driven inward into our deepest selves to find God. There is glory and might in this vital evanescence, this slow glacier-like flow of clothing and revealing matter, this ever uptossed rainbow of tangible humanity. It is no less of God's making than the spirit that is clothed therein.

We cannot yet have learned all that we are meant to learn through the body. How much of the teaching even of this world can the most diligent and most favoured man have exhausted before he is called to leave it! Is all that remains yet unlearned, unfelt, unexperienced to be lost? Who that has loved this earth can but believe that the spiritual body of which St. Paul speaks will be a yet *higher* channel of such revelation?

The meek who have found that their Lord spake true, and have indeed inherited the earth, who have seen that all matter is radiant of spiritual meaning, who would not cast a sigh after the loss of mere animal pleasure, would, I think, be the least willing to be without a body, to be unclothed without being again clothed upon.

Who, after centuries of glory in heaven, would not rejoice to behold once more that patient-headed child of winter and spring, the meek snowdrop? In whom, amidst the golden choirs, would not the vision of an old sunset wake such a song as the ancient dwellers of the earth would with gently flattened palm hush their throbbing harps to hear?

All this revelation, however, would render only *a* body necessary, not *this* body. The fullness of the word *resurrection* would hardly be met if this were all. We need not only a body to convey revelation to us but a body to reveal us to others. The thoughts, feelings, imaginations which arise in us must have their garments of revelation whereby shall be made manifest the unseen world *within us* to our brothers and sisters *around us*. Otherwise is each left in human loneliness.

Now, if this be one of the uses my body served on earth before, the new body must be like the old. More than that, it must be the same body, glorified as we are glorified, with all that was distinctive of each from his fellows *more* visible than ever before. The accidental, the nonessential, the unrevealing, the incomplete will have vanished. That which made the body what it was in the eyes of those who loved us will be tenfold there.

Will not this be the resurrection of the body—of the same body though not of the same dead matter? Every eye shall see the beloved, every heart will cry, *My own again!*—more mine because more himself than ever I beheld him!

For do we not say on earth, "He is not himself today," or, "She looks her own self." In other words, *She is more like herself than I have seen her for a long time.* And do we not express such thoughts when the heart is glad and the face is radiant? For we carry a better likeness of our friends in our hearts than their countenances, except at precious seasons, manifest outwardly to us.

Who will dare to call anything less than this a resurrection? Oh, how the letter kills! There are those who can believe that the dirt of their bodies will rise the same as it went down to the friendly grave, who yet doubt if they will know their friends when they rise again. And they call *that* believing in the resurrection!

What! Shall a man love his neighbour as himself, and then be content *not* to know him in heaven? Better be content to lose our consciousness altogether and know ourselves no longer either.

What! Shall God be the God of the families of the earth, and shall the love that he has thus created toward father and mother, brother and sister, wife and child, go moaning and longing to all eternity? Or worse, far worse, shall those loves die out of our bosoms? Shall God be God, and shall this be the end?

— NEW GARMENTS OF REVELATION —

Ah, my friends! What will resurrection or life be to me, how shall I continue to love God as I have learned to love him through you, if I find that he cares so little for this human heart of mine as to take from me the gracious visitings of your faces and forms?

True, I might have a gaze at Jesus now and then. But he would not be so good as I had thought him. And how should I see him if I could not see you? God will not take you, has not taken you from me to bury you out of my sight in the abyss of his own unfathomable being, where I cannot follow and find you, myself lost in the same awful gulf.

No, our God is an unveiling, a revealing God. He will raise you from the dead, that I may behold you. He will raise us all so that all loves which vanished from the earth may again stand forth, looking out again from the same eyes of eternal love and truth toward one another. He will raise us that you might hold out to me the same mighty hand of brotherhood, the same delicate and gentle yet strong hand of sisterhood—hold it out to this *me* that knew you and loved you in the days gone by.

I shall not care that the matter of the forms I loved a thousand years ago has returned to mingle with the sacred goings on of God's science, upon that far-off world wheeling its nursery of growing loves and wisdoms through space. I shall not care that the muscle which now sends the life-giving fluid through your heavenly veins is not formed of the very particles which once sent the blood to the pondering brain, the flashing eye, or the nervous right arm. I shall not care, I say, so long as it is *yourselves* that are before me, beloved.

So long as through these forms I know that, then I know that I look on my own, on the souls I loved of the ancient time. So long as my spirits have got garments of revealing after their own old lovely fashion, garments to reveal themselves to me, their forms will not matter to me.

The new shall then be dear as the old, and for the same reason, that it reveals the old love. And in the changes which, thank God, must take place when the mortal puts on immortality, shall we not feel that the nobler our friends are, the more they are themselves? Shall we not feel that the more the idea of each is carried out in the perfection of beauty, the more like they are to what we thought them in our most exalted moods? Will they not then be that which we saw in them in the rarest moments of profoundest communion? Will they not then be likest to that which we beheld through the veil of all their imperfections when we loved them the truest?

Lord, evermore give us this resurrection, like thine own in the body of thy transfiguration. Let us see, and hear, and know, and be seen, and heard, and known, as thou seest, hearest, and knowest. Give us glorified bodies through which to reveal the glorified thoughts which shall then inhabit us, when not only shalt thou reveal God, but each of us shall reveal thee.

And for this, Lord Jesus, come thou, the child, the obedient God, that we may be one with thee, and with every man and woman whom thou hast made, in the Father.

Insights Into

The God
of the Living

MICHAEL PHILLIPS

— WHAT KIND OF RESURRECTION BODY —

In one sense, MacDonald's sermon entitled "The God of the Living" (*Unspoken Sermons, First Series*) could more aptly have been called "The Resurrection of the Body." For the theme MacDonald here considers is not eternal life itself but what form that eternal life will take, a theme, as we saw, he echoed briefly in "Abba, Father." This he establishes early by clarifying that the Lord's argument with the Sadducees was no mere intellectual debate over life after death, but rather a discussion in which Jesus emphasized the *nature* of that life. It is a life, MacDonald is convinced, that will be a *bodily* one.

MacDonald phrases the fundamental question which is here under consideration as follows: "Let us inquire what is meant by the resurrection of the body. 'With what body do they come into the resurrection?'"

The nature of the resurrection life was always of intense interest to MacDonald. He held with a passion what some may find curious, that animals will partake in the resurrection, so much so that this belief contributed to the charges against him during his brief pastorate at Arundel that led to his ouster.

Why either he or his parishioners cared so vehemently about this relatively insignificant point of theological debate on which we can have no certain knowledge is a mystery. However, both sides did care. MacDonald let slip a few thoughts concerning animals in the afterlife in one of his sermons, outraging certain women of his congregation. The incident led to yet more dissatisfaction with his "orthodoxy" already being felt because of his wider and more imaginative views about God.

Yet perhaps this gives us a glimpse of MacDonald's conviction that the resurrection will be a bodily one. If it will not be physical in the same way in which this present material world is physical, perhaps it will be something *like* it, a new kind of physical, actual, real, tangible resurrection—with new glorified definitions to all such terms. How else than by such bodily means could animals *without* souls here on earth enter into that resurrection?

> Surely we are not required to believe that our same bodies are raised again. That is against science, common sense, and Scripture.... One feels

ashamed of arguing such a minor point. Who could wish his material body . . . to be fixed as his changeless possession, especially such as that body may be at the moment of death? Who would want such a body secured to him in worthless identity for the ages to come?

A man's material body will be to his consciousness at death no more than the old garment he throws aside at night, intending to put on a new and a better one in the morning. . . . As well might a Christian desire that the hair which has been shorn from him through all his past life should be restored to his risen and glorified head.

— THE PURPOSE OF THE BODY: REVELATION —

MacDonald suggests that the use of our present bodies in their earthly forms points to higher eternal purposes which must be fulfilled in the resurrection by new eternal bodies.

Let us first ask what is the use of this body of ours. Is it not the means of revelation to us, the *camera* in which God's eternal shows are set forth to our senses? It is by the body that we come into contact with Nature, with our fellow-men, with all their revelations of God to us. It is through the body that we receive all the lessons of passion, suffering, love, beauty, and science. It is through the body that we are both trained outward from ourselves and driven inward into our deepest selves to find God. There is glory and might in this vital . . . flow of clothing and revealing matter, this ever uptossed rainbow of tangible humanity. It is no less of God's making than the spirit that is clothed therein.

MacDonald then goes on to make a bold assertion, one upon which his thesis of a bodily resurrection is based. He says that there must be more that the body has to teach us than we can possibly learn in our earthly lifetime.

We cannot yet have learned all that we are meant to learn through the body. How much of the teaching even of this world can the most diligent and most favoured man have exhausted before he is called to leave it! Is all that remains yet unlearned, unfelt, unexperienced to be lost? Who that has loved this earth can but believe that the spiritual body of which St. Paul speaks will be a yet *higher* channel of such revelation? . . .

All this revelation, however, would render only *a* body necessary, not *this* body. The fullness of the word *resurrection* would hardly be met if this were all. We need not only a body to convey revelation to us but a body to reveal us to others. The thoughts, feelings, imaginations which arise in us must have their garments of revelation whereby shall be made manifest the unseen world *within us* to our brothers and sisters *around* us.

— NEW GARMENTS OF REVELATION —

Then MacDonald begins the inquiry toward which he has been leading. What kind of body will we have in

the next life? He says it will be the *same* body . . . yet
not the actual *material* body.

> The new body must be like the old. More than
> that, it must be the same body, glorified as we are
> glorified, with all that was distinctive of each from
> his fellows *more* visible than ever before. . . . That
> which made the body what it was in the eyes of
> those who loved us will be tenfold there.
>
> Will not this be the resurrection of the body—
> of the same body though not of the same dead mat-
> ter? Every eye shall see the beloved, every heart
> will cry, *My own again!*—more mine because more
> himself than ever I beheld him! . . .
>
> Who will dare to call anything less than this a
> resurrection? Oh, how the letter kills! There are
> those who can believe that the dirt of their bodies
> will rise the same as it went down to the friendly
> grave, who yet doubt if they will know their friends
> when they rise again. And they call *that* believing
> in the resurrection!
>
> What! Shall a man love his neighbour as him-
> self, and then be content *not* to know him in
> heaven?

MacDonald concludes with a striking vision of
heaven itself as old loves are rekindled. It will be filled,
he says, with visual and bodily recognition, with greet-
ings and expressions of love similar to such experiences
on earth, yet glorified and perfected once all differences,
imperfections, and unloves have vanished in the light of
eternity.

Ah, my friends! What will resurrection or life be to me, how shall I continue to love God as I have learned to love him through you, if I find that he cares so little for this human heart of mine as to take from me the gracious visitings of your faces and forms?

True, I might have a gaze at Jesus, now and then. But he would not be so good as I had thought him. And how should I see him if I could not see you?

This must be so, he says, because in all God does, revelation increases, not decreases. Thus, in eternity also every form of revelation must increase, and continue increasing forever.

Our God is an unveiling, a revealing God. He will raise you from the dead, that I may behold you. He will raise us all so that all loves which vanished from the earth may again stand forth, looking out again from the same eyes of eternal love and truth toward one another. He will raise us that you might hold out to me the same mighty hand of brother-hood, the same delicate and gentle yet strong hand of sisterhood—hold it out to this *me* that knew you and loved you in the days gone by. . . .

The new shall then be dear as the old, and for the same reason, that it reveals the old love. And in the changes which, thank God, must take place when the mortal puts on immortality, shall we not feel that the nobler our friends are, the more they are themselves? Shall we not feel that the more the idea of each is carried out in the perfection of beauty, the more like they are to what we thought them in our most exalted moods? . . . Will they not then be likest to that which we beheld through the veil of all their imperfections when we loved them the truest?

And finally, MacDonald ends with a prayer that, in its simple appeal for unity, cannot but remind us of Christ's own prayer in John 17, about which, as we read in chapter 1, MacDonald wrote, "The prayer of the Lord for unity between men and the Father and himself . . . the more I regard it, the more I am lost in the wonder and glory of the thing."

There can be no more fitting words with which to close than this quiet uplifting of MacDonald's heart in the same direction as his Lord's.

And for this, Lord Jesus, come thou, the child, the obedient God, that we may be one with thee, and with every man and woman whom thou hast made, in the Father.

Watch for future titles from Bethany House by George MacDonald and Michael Phillips. For more information about George MacDonald and Michael Phillips, see: *www.MacDonaldPhillips.com*

Don't miss *George MacDonald, Scotland's Beloved Storyteller*, by Michael Phillips.

For contact information, a complete listing of titles by Michael Phillips, and the availability of George Mac-Donald titles, both original and edited, write c/o:

Sunrise Books
P.O. Box 7003
Eureka, CA 95502
U.S.A.

Information on and subscriptions to the magazine *Leben* (issued quarterly)—dedicated to the spiritual vision of Michael Phillips and the legacy of George Mac-Donald—may also be obtained through the above address.

The Authors

George MacDonald (1824–1905), Scottish Victorian novelist, began his adult life as a clergyman and always considered himself a poet first of all. His unorthodox views resulted in a very short career in the pulpit in the early 1850s, after which he turned to writing in earnest. He initially attracted notice for poetry and his  adult fantasy, *Phantastes* (1855), but once he turned to the writing of realistic novels in the early 1860s, his name became widely known throughout Great Britain and the U.S. Over the next thirty years he wrote some 50 books, including, in addition to the novels, more poetry, short stories, fantasy, sermons, essays, and a full-length study of *Hamlet*. His influential body of work placed him alongside the great Victorian men of letters and his following was vast.

MacDonald died in 1905, and his reputation gradually declined in the twentieth century. Most of his books eventually went out of print as his name drifted from memory. A brief flurry of interest in his work was generated in 1924 at the centenary of his birth, resulting in several new editions of certain titles and the first major biography of his life, *George MacDonald and His Wife*, by his son Greville MacDonald.

Obscure though his name gradually became, however, MacDonald was read and revered by an impressive gallery of well-known figures, both in his own time and in the years since. A few of these include G. K. Chesterton (who called him "one of the three or four greatest men of the nineteenth century"), W. H. Auden (who said that MacDonald was "one of the most remarkable writers of the nineteenth century"), Oswald Chambers ("How I love that man!"), and most notably C. S. Lewis.

Lewis acknowledged his spiritual debt to MacDonald as so great that he published an entire anthology of quotations by MacDonald in hopes of turning the public toward his spiritual mentor in large numbers. In the introduction to that volume Lewis wrote:

> I dare not say that he is never in error; but to speak plainly I know hardly any other writer who seems to be closer, or more continually close, to the Spirit of Christ Himself. . . . I have never concealed the fact that I regarded him as my master; indeed I fancy I have never written a book in which I did not quote from him.

His efforts, however, were but modestly successful, and for the most part only in literary circles. Notwithstanding Lewis's laudatory words, MacDonald's name continued to fall out of the public consciousness. By the 1960s nearly all his work (except for a few stories and fairy tales) was out of print, though his inclusion, along with Lewis and his "inkling" friends, in the newly established Marion Wade Center at Wheaton College ensured that he would not be forgotten.

A resurgence of interest, primarily in the United States, began to mount in the 1970s and 1980s, given initial impetus by the work of Wheaton professor Dr. Rolland Hein and then exploding into public view from the efforts of MacDonald redactor and biographer Michael Phillips. Phillips' work resulted in new generations of readers discovering anew the treasures in MacDonald's work and led to a renewed publication of MacDonald's books on a scale not seen since his own lifetime.

MICHAEL PHILLIPS (B. 1946), Californian writer and novelist, is the man responsible for reawakening worldwide public interest in George MacDonald through publication of his edited and original editions of MacDonald's books. He is himself of Scottish descent, with distant links to the MacDonald clan.

Phillips first discovered MacDonald's work in the early 1970s. Dismayed to learn that all MacDonald's major fiction (as well as most other titles) was unavailable, Phillips embarked on an ambitious lifetime project to reintroduce the world to this remarkable author through many different means. Toward this end, he began to produce edited versions of MacDonald's dialect-heavy Scottish novels. The purpose of redacting these masterpieces was a practical one—hopefully to interest a contemporary publisher (skeptical about a dense five-hundred-page Victorian tome) to publish and promote them, and also to make MacDonald's stories and spiritual wisdom attractive and compelling to a new and less literarily patient reading audience.

Phillips began his initial editing of MacDonald's *Malcolm* in the mid–1970s. Though it took five years and rejections by thirty houses to find a publisher to believe with him that MacDonald could speak to new generations, the eventual publication of his redacted edition of *Malcolm* was so successful and was received so enthusiastically by the reading public and the MacDonald community, that it led to the eventual publication of eighteen redacted volumes that have to date sold over two million copies worldwide. The twentieth-century MacDonald renaissance had begun!

Over the next twenty years, Phillips expanded his efforts, producing original full-length editions of MacDonald's work to accompany the redacted novels, writing an acclaimed biography, *George MacDonald, Scotland's Beloved Storyteller*, and producing a series of books and studies about MacDonald.

During this time Phillips' stature as one of the leading Christian novelists of the late twentieth century was also rising. He penned dozens of novels of his own that were as well received as had been his work with MacDonald's, leading many to compare his output and spiritual insight and vision with that of his literary and spiritual mentor. More recently, Phillips has inaugurated the periodical *Leben* as yet one further means to keep the legacy of MacDonald alive, as well as to further his own spiritual vision. His tireless work on behalf of MacDonald has introduced countless thousands to the work of George MacDonald and ensured that coming generations never again forget the man whom, like C. S. Lewis before him, Phillips considers his spiritual and literary mentor. Though Phillips and his wife, Judy, alternate their time between the U.S. and Scotland, their home in Eureka, California, remains the base of their work.

Phillips is today generally recognized as one of the

foremost experts on MacDonald's life and work, a man with a keen insight into MacDonald's heart and message. He is widely regarded as the successor to MacDonald's vision and spiritual legacy for a new generation.

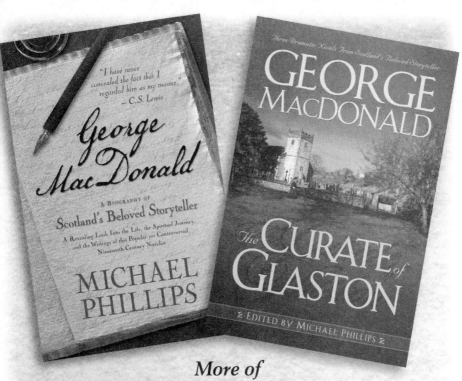

More of
George MacDonald

Scotland's Beloved Storyteller

George MacDonald, nineteenth-century Scottish novelist and poet, was reintroduced to twentieth-century readers by C. S. Lewis. Later in the century, Michael Phillips' vision, foresight, and editorial expertise ignited the MacDonald renaissance that we know today. In this extensive biography, Michael Phillips paints a revealing portrait of MacDonald, using the facts of his life to shape a picture of the man, set against the Scottish land he loved.

George MacDonald by Michael Phillips

Three Unforgettable Victorian Novels in One Edition

This trilogy depicts the spiritual awakening of curate Thomas Wingfold and the lives of those he touches. Surgeon Paul Faber believes in nothing but his own goodness until a beautiful patient reveals her secret past. Richard Tuke searches for the truth behind his mysterious heritage with the help of a thoughtful and independent woman. Filled with suspense and love, these novels reveal God's intimate and loving means of drawing hearts near.

The Curate of Glaston by George MacDonald

◆ BETHANY HOUSE